LAW
in the
SCHOOL

A Guide for California Schools,
School Safety Personnel and
Law Enforcement

Sixth Edition

August 2000

California Department of Justice
Bill Lockyer, Attorney General

ISBN 0-8011-9718-X

Additional copies of Law in the School can be purchased through the
California Department of Education, at:

CDE Press
1-800-995-4099

or by writing to:

CDE Press
California Department of Education
P.O. Box 944272
Sacramento, CA 94244-2720

Preface

Our children's future and that of our state depend upon making *every* school campus a safe learning environment. School officials have a duty to act quickly and wisely when crime or violence occurs on campus. To do this, however, school staff must have confidence in their knowledge of the law.

It is with great pleasure that I present to you the Sixth Edition of *Law in the School*. This handbook is a guide to assist teachers, administrators, law enforcement and school security personnel in carrying out their responsibility to provide a safe school environment. As Attorney General, I have made school safety a top priority by updating and republishing this valuable reference tool for educators, law enforcement and other community leaders. I hope we can help make our schools even safer.

This edition features the most current laws and court decisions that will help school officials understand how to deal with criminal activities affecting our schools. It includes important information on issues ranging from truancy to weapons on campus.

In order to ensure the basic constitutional right of California children to attend schools that are safe and secure, in 1983 the Attorney General and the State Superintendent of Public Instruction created a formal partnership to encourage law enforcement agencies and schools to develop and implement interagency collaborations to promote safe schools, improve school attendance and encourage good citizenship. Today, we are working harder than ever to strengthen our partnership. In June 2000, the Safe Schools Task Force we established last year issued its final report, with eight recommendations and 46 strategies to improve school safety. Through our partnership we also developed the *Crisis Response Box — Partnering for Safe Schools*, a guide to assist schools in crisis prevention planning.

We must also address the underlying causes of violence, such as abuse and trauma in early childhood; and early patterns of problem behavior, such as truancy, vandalism and substance abuse — to prevent youth from turning to more serious crime. Every first-, second- or third-grade teacher can spot youngsters in the classroom who will turn out to be problem kids. Input from those teachers would assist greatly in identifying early signs of gang or drug problems. Working together, law enforcement, school officials, parents and health and social services professionals can address the core issues relating to youth violence and form a strong network for intervention and prevention.

It is my hope that *Law in the School* serves as a valuable resource for you, your campus and your community. Only in a safe environment can schools foster the academic excellence so important to our children and our future.

BILL LOCKYER
Attorney General

Table of Contents

How to Use This Handbook

Law in the School was developed to help school teachers, administrators, school safety personnel and criminal justice agencies in their efforts to secure a safe school environment — a right guaranteed by the California Constitution.

The goal in making this handbook available is to provide a better understanding of state and federal laws that specifically relate to establishing and maintaining safe schools. School rules and local and district ordinances that apply to school operations (often found in local or district publications) and many state and federal laws unrelated to safety have not been included.

The following information explains the various citations used throughout this publication.

Statutes

Both the U.S. Congress and the California Legislature enact statutes or laws. Federal statutes appear as follows: 20 U.S.C., §§ 4071-4074. This refers to a statute found in the 20th volume of the U.S. Code, beginning at section 4071.

State statutes are listed as follows: Gov. Code, § 53069.5. This refers to a statute that can be found in the California Government Code, section 53069.5. If the "53069.5" were followed by the term "*et seq.*," it would mean a citation from section 53069.5 and the sections that follow.

Regulations

Federal and state agencies adopt regulations to interpret and enforce statutes. Federal regulation citations are written: 34 C.F.R. § 99.

This citation refers to the 34th volume of the Code of Federal Regulations (C.F.R.), beginning at section 99.

California regulations are listed in this way: Title 5, Cal. Code of Regs., § 5530. This citation refers to Title 5 of the California Code of Regulations, section 5530. The California Code of Regulations was previously known as the California Administrative Code and may occasionally be cited in this manner.

Court Cases

Courts of law make decisions about whether certain actions constitute a violation of the law and whether or not particular laws are constitutional. The U.S. Supreme Court is the highest court in the country, while the California Supreme Court is the highest court in the state.

U.S. Supreme Court citations appear as follows: *New Jersey v. T.L.O.* (1985) 469 U.S. 325, 83 L.Ed.2d 720, 105 S.Ct. 733. *T.L.O.* was decided in 1985. The citation refers to volume 469 of the U.S. Reports, beginning on page 325; or volume 83 of the Lawyer's Edition, Second Series, beginning on page 720; or volume 105 of the Supreme Court Reports, beginning on page 733.

California Supreme Court cases are listed in this way: *In re Michael G.* (1988) 44 Cal.3d 283. *In re Michael G.* was decided in 1988. The citation refers to volume 44 of the California Reports, Third Series, beginning on page 283.

California Courts of Appeal citations are written: *Lucas v. Fresno Unified School District* (1993) 14 Cal.App.4th 66. *Fresno Unified* was decided in 1993. The citation refers to volume 14 of the California Appellate Reports, Fourth Series, beginning on page 66.

American Law Reports are listed: Annotation 36 A.L.R.3d 330, 340. Annotated cases are found in the American Law Reports (A.L.R.). This case refers to the 36th volume, Third Series, found on pages 330 and 340.

California Attorney General Opinions

There are occasional references to California Attorney General Opinions, which are written in response to questions by state legislators or other public officials or agencies about the legality of a particular object or action. The opinions are advisory only and *do not* constitute the law of the state or action.

These citations appear as follows: 75 Ops.Cal.Atty.Gen. 155 (1990). This opinion was written in 1990. The reference is to the 75th volume of the Opinions of the California Attorney General, beginning on page 155.

The California Attorney General Opinion's Unit has established a Web site. The address is http://caag.state.ca.us./opinions. This site included opinions published from 1997 to the present. It provides access to the monthly opinion report, information on who may request an opinion, *Quo Warranto* applications and frequently asked questions.

For More Information

This handbook is not intended as a substitute for legal advice from a county council, agency attorney, private attorney or district attorney. School administrators, school security personnel or teachers having specific legal questions or problems interpreting a statute, court case or opinion should seek legal assistance from one of the resources listed above.

This publication is current through January 2000 with respect to statutes, case law and Attorney General Opinions.

The Duty to Protect Students

In 1982, California voters amended the state Constitution by adding the "Right to Safe Schools" provision which states: All students and staff of primary, elementary, junior high and senior high schools have the inalienable right to attend campuses which are safe, secure and peaceful." (Cal. Const., art. I, § 28, subd. (c).)[1]

This chapter discusses this important right in conjunction with the state-mandated duties of school officials and personnel to: develop comprehensive safe school plans, conduct criminal background checks, provide adequate supervision for students and, report criminal acts committed by students and abusive actions taken against them.

The Right to Safe Schools

Since 1982, attorneys and legal scholars have debated how to implement California's constitutional right to safe schools. Some urged that litigants could sue for damages based solely on this right. Others argued that further enabling language was necessary to describe a process for such lawsuits. *(Hosemann v. Oakland Unified School District* (1989) unpublished opinion (1st Dist., Div. 3, (#A035856) May 30, 1989.)

In 1988, the issue was finally resolved in the *Leger v. Stockton Unified School District* case. The Court of Appeal held that Article I,

---

[1] For a discussion of this constitutional right, see Kimberly A. Sawyer, *The Right to Safe Schools: A Newly Recognized Inalienable Right,* Pacific Law Journal, 14 (1983) 1309; and Stuart Biegel, *The Safe Schools Provision: Can a Nebulous Constitutional Right Be a Vehicle for Change?* Hastings Constitutional Law Quarterly, 14 (1987) 789.

section 28, subdivision (c) is not "self-executing" in the sense of supplying a right to sue for damages. (*Leger v. Stockton Unified School District* (1988) 202 Cal.App.3d 1448.) The court decision expresses a general right without specifying any rules for its enforcement. It imposes no mandatory duties to make a school safe which would give rise to constitutional liability. However, schools have a duty to use reasonable care to protect students from known or foreseeable dangers. If staff fail to provide such care, the district and its employees can be held liable using traditional civil law tort remedies. (Gov. Code, §§ 820, 815.2.)

Even though the "Right to Safe Schools" provision does not support constitutional lawsuits, it stands as a declaration of rights. It is mandatory that all government agencies comply with it. Schools are required to recognize that all students and staff have the right to attend safe campuses and are prohibited from taking official actions that contradict the provisions of Article 1, section 28(c). (*Leger v. Stockton Unified School District, supra.*)

Rethinking Our Strategies

In response to the challenge of creating safer schools and protecting children's welfare, school districts, law enforcement agencies, courts and community organizations are rethinking their working relationships. Successfully addressing the challenges related to school and community violence prevention requires the efforts of multiple agencies. Limited fiscal and personnel resources must be utilized effectively to fill the increasing demand and scope for services.

It is now common practice for schools to work closely with many agencies in developing and implementing prevention, intervention and enforcement activities. Everyone involved — parents, school administrators, teachers, staff, students, criminal justice professionals and youth-serving agencies — are being required to take a new look at the relationships between students, staff and the community at

2

every stage of planning and intervention. Above all, the challenge of providing safe schools is, at its core, a people challenge.[2]

Individual Rights vs. Safety

Ever-changing case law and emerging legal trends are also redefining the unique relationships within the schools. In order to establish safer schools, it is essential to dispel folklore, acknowledge current realities and balance individual rights with the need to ensure order and safety. To achieve these goals, the following four concepts should be considered:

- Relationships of trust between students and staff.
- Knowledge of students' and staffs' civil rights and personal responsibility.
- Duty to protect.
- "Acting under the color of authority."

Relationships of trust between students and staff. First, compulsory education laws create a special relationship between students and staff. The law compels students to attend school; the law requires parents to send their children to school. Students have a *constitutional* guarantee to a safe, secure and peaceful school environment. If school officials do not acknowledge unsafe conditions, then they have failed to guarantee safe surroundings in an environment from which students are not free to leave.

Student/staff civil rights and personal responsibility. The second issue involves safe school decisions and policies affecting students' and staff's civil rights. The First and Fourth Amendments of the U.S. Constitution address free speech issues and searches and seizures. Schools must consider these constitutional guarantees when developing and enforcing policies. Additionally, when students

---

[2] *Safe Schools: A Planning Guide for Action,* Sacramento: California Department of Education, Safe Schools and Violence Prevention Office; Office of the Attorney General, Crime and Violence Prevention Center, 1995.

and staff members have been injured on campus either by violence or falling down on the blacktop, they have effectively challenged school district safety policies and procedures due to the Federal Civil Rights Act, section 1983 and the 14th Amendment (right to due process).

Duty to protect. Third, each school has a duty to protect students and staff. Schools must provide adequate campus supervision. Rules, policies and procedures alone will not exempt the school district or staff members from legal action by students or other people injured on campuses (even from students who are minors). Minors can be impulsive; they do not always consider the consequences of their actions. Therefore, school officials must be vigilant in seeing that campus supervision is sufficient to ensure safety.

"Acting under the color of authority." The final consideration affecting students/staff relationships, "acting under the color of authority," involves situations in which school staff command students to follow orders given by an authority figure. Within the school environment, "color of authority" refers specifically to the real or implied authority granted to a school staff member through the governing board and how the student perceives and responds to the staff's authority. Any direction given to students must be lawful, whether or not the students comply. "Acting under the color of authority," adults must act fairly, legally, responsibly and respectfully towards each other and their students. If school staff are unreasonable and abuse their authority, this may lead to the school being drawn into unnecessary and expensive litigation. This may also lead to decreased morale and increased disciplinary problems for staff and students.

Two premises form the cornerstone of school safety:
- A responsible alliance between the schools and law enforcement working with other community partners as appropriate, is essential in carrying out the four concepts listed above.[3]

---

[3] Ops.Cal.Atty.Gen., Supp. Appen. to J. of Assembly, Reg. Sess. 87 (1969).

- The goal of education is to educate and foster student intelligence and critical decision making, personal dignity, integrity and independence so that the need for outer restraints diminishes as responsible citizenship develops.

These ideas are consistent with federal legislation, the Goals 2000: Educate America Act. Goal 7 of the Act, "Safe, Disciplined, and Alcohol- and Drug-Free Schools," states, in part, that "Maintaining a disciplined environment conducive to learning does not necessarily mean adopting tough policies to keep students silent in their seats. To improve student academic performance, the key is to create an atmosphere in which students and teachers are engaged in learning and where misbehavior is dealt with quickly, firmly, and fairly. A learning environment requires an ethic of caring that shapes staff-student relationships." (Public Law 103-227 (March 31, 1994), §§ 102, 108 Stat. 130.)

Safe School Planning

When educators, law enforcement, parents, students and youth-serving agency personnel work together to develop an action plan for reducing the threat or reality of criminal incidents on school campuses, they enhance school safety. Their efforts help create and maintain an orderly, purposeful school environment where students and staff are able to learn and teach.

Since 1982, the courts and the Legislature have attempted to implement section 28(c) — The Right To Safe Schools — and have supported safe school plans as a positive strategy to meet the constitutional guarantee.

In 1983, the California Attorney General and the State Superintendent of Public Instruction formed a partnership between the Department of Justice and the California Department of Education to provide statewide guidance on developing school safety strategies. The program was endorsed in 1985 by the Legislature and the Governor with enactment of the Interagency School Safety Demonstration Act, also known as the School/Law Enforcement Partnership Program. (Ed. Code, §§ 32260-32295.) (For more information on this Partnership, refer to: http://www.cde.ca.gov/spbranch/safety/.)

In October 1997, the Governor signed into law legislation making each school district and county office of education responsible for the overall development of comprehensive safe school plans for its schools operating any kindergarten and any grades 1 to 12, inclusive. Each school site was required to adopt a comprehensive school safety plan by September 1, 1998. (Ed. Code, § 35294.1 *et seq.*) The comprehensive safety plan must identify appropriate strategies and programs that will provide or maintain a high level of school safety and address the school's procedures for complying with existing laws.

As a continuing incentive for schools to develop their individual safety plans, the School/Law Enforcement Partnership awards matching mini-grants for implementation of a portion of each existing comprehensive plan under the "Safe School Plan Implementation Grant Program." In conjunction with the grant program, the Partnership provides statewide safe schools training to any school district personnel wishing to develop and implement a safe school plan. Since 1989, the Partnership has averaged 20 safe schools training workshops per year. A select group of 30 professional school and law enforcement members have been specially trained to lead the workshops.[4]

Schools should begin developing their comprehensive school safety plans by thoroughly reviewing current crime reports and disciplinary actions. These reports should reflect unlawful activities and potential problems. The school safety planning process should identify appropriate strategies and programs that will provide or maintain a high level of school safety. Once written, the comprehensive school safety plan shall be evaluated and amended, as needed, by the

---

[4] Check the Safe Schools and Violence Prevention Office web site for current grant and training information: http://www.cde.ca.gov/spbranch/safety/

school safety planning committee no less than once a year to ensure that the plan is properly implemented. (Ed. Code, § 35294.2.)

The School/Law Enforcement Partnership has developed a planning guide that helps schools formulate their plans.[5] School officials should not limit the planning process when developing their plans. A comprehensive school safety plan should, at a minimum, state the laws, board policies and regulations for student, parent, staff and visitor conduct in and around the school campus and during school-sponsored activities. School officials should tailor each safety plan to the unique needs of the individual school.

The Partnership has designed a "Seven Step" planning process for developing comprehensive safe school plans.[6] The Partnership recommends that school safety teams utilize these steps when developing their plans: 1) identify safe school planning committee members; 2) create a vision for the school; 3) gather and analyze information about the school and its community; 4) identify school's and community's areas of desired change; 5) set major goals; 6) select and implement strategies for each safe school component; and, 7) evaluate and assess progress.

Staff Training

Once the interagency school safety plan is developed and implemented, it is highly recommended that all staff become thoroughly familiar with the plan and receive training in school safety. Cross-training with other agencies is a useful technique. All school employees (principals, security staff, teachers, aides, custodians, clerical and health workers, substitutes, bus drivers and others) must be aware of their individual responsibility for creating and maintaining a safe campus. Students, parents and community members should receive training that focuses on their roles in creating a positive, safe

---

[5] *Safe Schools: A Planning Guide for Action,* Sacramento: California Department of Education, Safe Schools and Violence Prevention Office; Office of the Attorney General, Crime and Violence Prevention Center, 1995.

[6] *Ibid.*

educational environment. Whenever possible, educators and law enforcement officers should attend juvenile legal updates and school safety conferences.

Additionally, educators and law enforcement officers can better protect students and staff from harm by keeping current on school safety legislation, court decisions and statewide school safety programs that prevent injuries, crimes and litigation. Schools should develop school safety resource libraries that include books, web sites or Internet locations, videotapes, pamphlets and information on model programs. Schools should make these materials available for staff training and review.

Criminal Background Checks and Employment of Certificated and Classified Employees

In 1997, California enacted two laws that impose significant obligations on school districts and county offices of education to review the criminal history of applicants and current employees.

California law now prohibits school entities from hiring any school employee until the Department of Justice (DOJ) completes a background check to determine if the applicant has an arrest or criminal history. Under the law, DOJ must complete the fingerprint check and return its findings to the district within 15 working days after receiving the identification cards. Once an electronic fingerprinting system is fully implemented with terminals statewide, the check must be completed within three working days. If DOJ cannot complete the check within that time, it must notify the district by phone and confirm in writing. The district cannot employ the applicant until DOJ completes its check. (Ed. Code, § 45125, subds. (a), (b), & (c).)

This law eliminated the exception for substitute and temporary personnel regardless of length of employment, and prohibits the employment of any person in any classified position until DOJ

8

completes its check. This statute does not apply to secondary pupils who are to be employed in a temporary or part-time position at the school that they attend. (Ed. Code, § 45125, subds. (c) & (g).)

The legislation further requires criminal background checks of employees of school contractors who will have any contact with pupils while providing the following or similar services: janitorial, administrative, landscape, transportation or food-related. This does not apply in "emergency or exceptional" situations, such as when pupil health or safety is endangered, or when the district determines that the employees will have limited contact with students, considering the following specified factors: length of time contractors are on campus, whether students will be in proximity with the work site and whether the contractors will be working by themselves or with others. In those cases, school districts must take appropriate steps to protect the safety of any pupil that may come in contact with these employees. (Ed. Code, § 45125.1, subds. (a), (b), & (c).)

A contractor must not allow any employee to have contact with pupils until the background check has been completed, and must certify in writing to the district that none of its employees who may come in contact with pupils have been convicted of a felony as defined in Education Code section 45122.1. The contractor must provide the names of employees who may come in contact with pupils to the school district who shall then provide the relevant lists of employees to the appropriate schools within its jurisdiction. An entity having a contract as specified in subdivision (a) of section 45125.1 on the effective date of this section must complete the requirements of this section within 90 days of that date. (Ed. Code, § 45125.1, subds. (e), (f), & (g).)

County boards of education and school districts must, prior to issuing a temporary certificate, obtain a criminal record summary of the applicant and may not issue a temporary certificate if the applicant has been convicted of a violent or serious felony. (Ed. Code, §§ 44332, 44332.5, 44332.6.)

The Commission on Teacher Credentialing must deny the credential application of any person who has been convicted of a serious or violent felony, and must revoke the credential of any person convicted of such crimes. (Ed. Code, § 44346.1.)

School districts are prohibited from employing or retaining in employment, any person in a position requiring a credential (or supervising positions requiring credentials), if that person has been convicted of a violent or serious felony and is a temporary or substitute employee, or is a probationary employee prior to March 15 of his or her second probationary year. When the district receives a confirming letter from DOJ, the employee is terminated automatically unless the employee challenges the criminal record. If DOJ withdraws its letter, the employee is immediately reinstated with back pay and benefits. This section also applies to charter schools. (Ed. Code, § 44830.1.)

Persons convicted of violent or serious felonies are prohibited from being employed in classified positions. A district may not retain a current temporary, substitute or probationary classified employee who has been convicted of such crimes. (Ed. Code, § 45122.1.) As with section 44830.1(e), upon telephone or electronic mail notice of the conviction, the district must immediately suspend the employee without pay. Once the district receives written verification, the employee is automatically dismissed. Employees can challenge the criminal record, and if the DOJ notice is withdrawn, the employee must be reinstated with back pay and benefits.

"Violent" felonies are listed in Penal Code section 667.5 and include: murder; voluntary manslaughter; mayhem; rape; sodomy or oral copulation by force; lewd acts on a child under 14; any felony punishable by death or life in prison; any felony involving the infliction of great bodily injury on another; robbery of an inhabited dwelling; arson; attempted murder; kidnaping; continuous sexual abuse of a child; and, carjacking.

"Serious" felonies are listed in Penal Code section 1192.7 and include: murder; voluntary manslaughter; mayhem; rape; sodomy or oral copulation by force; lewd or lascivious acts on a child under 14; any felony punishable by death or life in prison; any felony involving the infliction of great bodily injury on another; attempted murder; assault with the intent to commit rape or robbery; assault with a deadly weapon on a peace officer; arson; exploding a destructive device causing great bodily injury or mayhem; exploding a destructive device with intent to murder; burglary of an inhabited dwelling; robbery or bank robbery; kidnaping; selling or giving heroin, cocaine, PCP, or methamphetamine-related drug; grand theft involving a firearm; and, carjacking.

In all of the situations described in Education Code section 44008, employment cannot be denied or terminated solely on the basis of the conviction if the person has obtained a certificate of rehabilitation and pardon under the Penal Code. Additionally, such employment cannot be denied or terminated if the person can prove to the sentencing court that he or she has been rehabilitated for purposes of school employment for at least one year. (Pen. Code, § 4852.01; Ed. Code, § 44332.)

Electronic Fingerprinting

DOJ has implemented a statewide electronic fingerprinting system known as "Live Scan."[7] DOJ, in conjunction with the California State Sheriff's Association, as of July 2000, has 183 terminals operational throughout the state. All 58 counties have at least one terminal in operation. The terminals are installed in local law enforcement agencies, university or college police departments, county offices of education, school districts and city government buildings. This system is designed to expedite school and law enforcement fingerprint application requests. (Refer to http://caag.state.ca.us/app/contact.pdf. for locations and hours on the terminal closest to you.)

---

[7] California Department of Justice, Applicant Fingerprint Submissions, Live Scan web site: http://caag.state.ca.us/app/

Live Scan technology replaces the process of recording an individual's fingerprint patterns by hand. Digitizing the fingerprint minutiae (the characteristics that make fingerprints unique) enables the electronic transfer of the fingerprint image data, in combination with personal data information, to central site computers at DOJ in a matter of seconds rather than days required to submit a hard copy. Once at DOJ, the applicant-related information is processed electronically. If no prior record is found, the requesting agency will be notified. If the applicant is found to have a prior criminal record, the automated information is forwarded to the Applicant Response Unit. This unit reviews and compares the new, incoming application against the criminal record, and determines what information is legally authorized to disseminate.

The DOJ fingerprint applicant process is fully automated. If applicants utilize this process, up to 95% of electronic applicant fingerprint submissions will be processed in 72 hours or less. However, 5% of the submissions must be manually processed to ensure accuracy and cross-check information. DOJ will also interface with and forward fingerprints to the Federal Bureau of Investigation (if required).

School Volunteers

School districts, county offices of education and private schools may request DOJ to provide criminal offense information on prospective volunteers. In addition, school districts and county offices of education may also request that DOJ provide subsequent arrest notification service. (Ed. Code, § 35021.2; Pen. Code, § 11105.2.)

Duty to Supervise Students

In 1970, the California Supreme Court declared that "California law has long imposed on school authorities a duty to supervise . . . the conduct of children on the school grounds and to enforce those rules and regulations necessary to their protection. . . . Such regulation is necessary precisely because of the commonly known tendency of students to engage in aggressive and impulsive behavior which exposes them and their peers to serious physical harm."[8]

State law requires teachers to "enforce . . . the rules and regulations prescribed for schools." (Ed. Code, § 44805.) The code further specifies that teachers and administrators must exercise reasonable control over students, but may only use physical control as is "reasonably necessary to maintain order, protect property, or protect the health and safety of pupils, or to maintain proper and appropriate conditions conducive to learning. . . . " (Ed. Code, § 44807.)

Rules and regulations prescribed for schools by the California Department of Education provide the following: "All certificated personnel shall exercise careful supervision of the moral conditions in their respective schools. . . . " (Title 5, California Code of Regulations, section 5530.) The principal is required to provide playground supervision before and after school as well as during recess and other scheduled breaks. The duty to supervise extends beyond the classroom and is required at special school activities, athletic events and school field trips.[9]

While teachers are not required to "police" the pathway to and from schools, they must take appropriate action to see that students are ultimately held accountable for their behavior. Education Code section 44807 states that "every teacher in the public schools shall hold pupils to a strict account for their conduct on the way to and from school, on the playgrounds, or during recess." (*Torsiello v. Oakland Unified School District* (1987) 197 Cal.App.3d 41, 45, review den.)

---

[8] *Daily v. Los Angeles Unified School District* (1970) 2 Cal.3d 741, 747-748; *Bartell v. Palos Verdes Peninsula School District* (1978) 83 Cal.App.3d 492, 499-500. The duty of supervision, however, does not require "round-the-clock" supervision of school premises and is "limited to school-related or encouraged functions and to activities taking place during school hours."

[9] Cal. Code of Regs., tit. 5, §§ 5531, 5552. *Castro v. Los Angeles Board of Education* (1976) 54 Cal.App.3d 232; *Torsiello v. Oakland Unified School District* (1987) 197 Cal.App.3d 371; *Iverson v. Muroc Unified School District*. (App. 5 Dist. 1995) 38 Cal.Rptr.2d 35.

However, Education Code section 44808 exempts school personnel from responsibility or liability for the safety or conduct of students off school property unless school personnel are negligent, or the school has sponsored an off-campus activity or provided transportation for students to and from school premises. For example, if the school is negligent in failing to provide a reasonably safe bus transportation system, then liability may result. In short, when carrying out their duty to supervise students, school officials effectively take the place of parents and are responsible for actively protecting the children under their charge. (*Stuart v. Board of Education (1911) 161 Cal. 210, 213; People v. Curtiss* (1931) 116 Cal.App.Supp. 771, 775.)

Adult Supervision

School safety and discipline require adult supervision. Adults must be present to properly monitor students, prevent or correct harmful situations or call for help when a situation is beyond their control.

Schools cannot escape liability simply because specific dangers to students were unforeseen. Additionally, schools may be held accountable if danger can be anticipated and supervision is deemed necessary to avoid that danger, but is not provided. (36 A.L.R.3d 330, 340.)

Failure to provide any supervision. Staff members have a duty to be present and, whenever possible, prevent accidents that can occur while children are together. Case law illustrates that administrators are required to do more than assign staff. The principal has a duty to ensure that personnel are actually on hand and supervising students.

In *Ziegler v. Santa Cruz City High School District*, a student was sitting on a railing near a stairwell when another student suddenly pushed him. The victim fell off the railing and was killed by the fall. Although staff had warned students not to sit on the railing, the school had not assigned a staff person to supervise students when they used the stairs. The court of appeals held that this was sufficient justification for a jury finding of negligence on the part of the school. (*Ziegler v. Santa Cruz City High School District* (1959) 168 Cal.App.2d 277.)

In *Forgnone v. Salvador Union Elementary School District*, a student's arm was broken in a classroom scuffle with another student during the lunch period. Since no teacher was present in the classroom at the time of the incident, the court held this sufficient to support a claim of negligence against the district. (*Forgnone v. Salvador Union Elementary School District* (1940) 41 Cal.App.2d 423.)[10]

Failure to provide enough supervision. Even when a supervising teacher is present and conscientiously overseeing student activities, it is clear that one individual cannot be everywhere at once. Therefore, school authorities must provide sufficient supervisory personnel in given areas to improve staff response time in potentially dangerous situations. School authorities may be considered negligent if they fail to provide adequate staff.

For example, in the case of *Charonnat v. San Francisco Unified School District*, only one teacher was assigned to supervise 150 elementary students in the schoolyard during lunch. When a student's leg was broken in a fight, the jury's finding of inadequate supervision was held to be justified. (*Charonnat v. San Francisco Unified School District* (1943) 56 Cal.App.2d 840.)

Failure to supervise diligently. It is not enough that teachers are assigned to supervise students; they must conscientiously and actively carry out their supervisory duties.

In *Dailey v. Los Angeles Unified School District*, a teacher on supervisory playground duty sat in his office with his back to the playground, talking on the telephone and preparing lesson plans. Two students got into a friendly "slap fight." One student fell after being hit, fracturing his skull on the asphalt pavement. He died later that night. The California Supreme Court held that a finding of inadequate supervision was justified. The fact that both students

---

[10] See also *Beck v. San Francisco, etc., School District* (1964) 225 Cal.App.2d 503; *Tymkowicz v. San Jose Unified School District* (1957) 151 Cal.App.2d 517.

willingly, even negligently, engaged in the fight was no defense. The teacher had a duty to protect the students from their own impulses or aggression. (*Dailey v. Los Angeles Unified School District* (1970) 2 Cal.3d 741.)

In *Lucas v. Fresno Unified School District*, a child injured while throwing dirt clods during recess was allowed to sue the school district. The Court of Appeal held that the district had a duty to supervise the child and his classmates, even though the student knew that throwing dirt clods was wrong and purposely engaged in the activity. (*Lucas v. Fresno Unified School District* (1993) 14 Cal.App.4th 866.)

In *Lilienthal v. San Leandro Unified School District*, a student in a metal crafts class was struck in the eye by a knife-shaped metal piece thrown by a classmate. The incident occurred during class in the presence of the teacher. Apparently, some of the students had been flipping the object into the ground for more than 30 minutes. The teacher maintained that he had not seen the students playing with the object. Nevertheless, evidence that students had been throwing around a potentially dangerous metal piece for some time before the accident justified a verdict that the teacher's failure to discover and stop the conduct constituted negligence. (*Lilienthal v. San Leandro Unified School District* (1956) 139 Cal.App.2d 453; *Charonnat v. San Francisco Unified School District, supra.*)

In *Hoyem v. Manhattan Beach City School District*, a 10-year-old boy left school before the end of his scheduled classes. At a public intersection, the boy was struck by a motorcycle and seriously injured. The California Supreme Court held that if the school district failed to exercise ordinary care in supervising the student while on school premises, and if this failure caused the injuries, the school district might be held responsible. In the Hoyem case, the trial court ultimately ruled that the school district had exercised ordinary care in its supervision of the boy and could not be held liable. (*Hoyem v. Manhattan Beach City School District* (1978) 22 Cal.3d 508.)

The duty to act. While the presence of school personnel will often prevent trouble, staff also should recognize and respond to dangerous situations. Staff cannot ignore or minimize problems, nor can they rationalize inaction. A teacher, security staff person or administrator must act effectively and quickly or call for help.

An example of this school duty to act was posed in the case of *Biggers v. Sacramento City Unified School District*, in which a gang of 10 to 15 juveniles — without provocation — attacked a high school student exiting a restroom. The student was knocked uncon-scious and seriously injured. The Court of Appeal held that if school authorities knew gangs were endangering students and "just turned their backs to the whole problem," the school could not escape liability. (*Biggers v. Sacramento City Unified School District* (1972) 25 Cal.App.3d 269.)

In *Peterson v. San Francisco Community College District*, the Califor-nia Supreme Court held that the district had a duty to exercise due care to protect students attending community college classes and activities from reasonably foreseeable assault. The district was held to be in a superior position to know about crimes occurring on campus and to protect students from repeated incidents. (*Peterson v. San Francisco Community College District* (1984) 36 Cal.3d 799.)

In *Peterson*, the court held that a college might be liable for a sexual assault where untrimmed foliage around a stairway allowed an assailant to lie in wait for victims. However, where there is not a meaningful causal connection between failing to fix a shattered light bulb in a darkened stairwell and a sexual assault begun by the appellant's acquaintances in a dormitory room, the school was not held liable. (*Tanja H. v. Regents of the University of California* (1991) 228 Cal.App.3d 434, 438.)

In *Constantinescu v. Conejo Valley Unified School District*, the Court of Appeal found that the duty of caring for students extended to maintaining a nearby parking lot in safe condition, even if the school district did not own the lot. In this case, children were injured after a car accelerated and jumped the parking lot curb. The court ruled against the school district because its administrators knew, or should have known, that the parking lot was a busy and dangerous place.

They could have taken steps — the erection of traffic barriers, for example — to protect students. The district had, in part, created the danger when it earlier converted a bus loading zone to a different use without regard to traffic patterns. The court found that this outweighed the fact the school did not own or directly control the property where the children were injured. (*Constantinescu v. Conejo Valley Unified School District* (1993) 16 Cal.App.4th 1466.)

In *Rodriguez v. Inglewood Unified School District*, the Court of Appeal stated, "A special relationship is formed between a school district and its students so as to impose an affirmative duty on the district to take all reasonable steps to protect its students." (*Rodriguez v. Inglewood Unified School District* (1986) 186 Cal.App.3d 707.)

In this, as in all of the cases cited above, the point was made that every school staff person is responsible for recognizing and responding effectively to any known dangers on school grounds.

School District Police, Security Departments and Volunteers

Many communities and school districts have sustained significant financial losses through vandalism and suffered through the trauma resulting from school crime and violence. In order to create healthier and safer schools, some communities and districts have established school district police or security forces and have requested parent volunteers to help on campus and at school-related events.

The California Education Code authorizes every public school district board of education to establish either a school district police department or security department. In all matters, the Legislature intended that school police and school security officers be supplementary to local law enforcement agencies and did not vest them with general police powers. (Ed. Code, § 39670; 58 Ops.Cal.Atty.Gen. 363 (1975).)

School Police

The governing board of any school district may establish a security department or a police department. School police officers, employed by a school district police department, are peace officers for the purpose of carrying out their duty according to statutory limitations. (Pen. Code, § 830.32; Ed. Code, §§ 39670-39671.)

School police officers are authorized to investigate criminal activity that occurs on school district property and make arrests for public offenses when there is immediate danger to people or property, or of the perpetrator's escape. Their primary duty is to ensure student and staff safety as well as the security of school property belonging to school personnel. School peace officers may carry firearms "only if authorized by and under such terms and conditions as are specified by their employing agency [school district]." (Pen. Code, § 830.32.)

Legislation enacted in 1998 provides specific criteria for fingerprinting and training of school police personnel by specified dates. Every school peace officer first employed by a K-12 public school district before July 1, 1999, shall, in order to retain his or her conditions of employment, submit his or her fingerprints to DOJ, and be a person who is not prohibited from employment by a school district. DOJ shall forward the fingerprints to the Federal Bureau of Investigation. Additionally, any school district police officer employed after January 1, 1975, shall successfully complete a training course prescribed by the Commission on Peace Officer Standards and Training (POST) before exercising the powers of a peace officer, except while participating in a POST approved supervised field training program. Each police chief, or any other person in charge of a local law enforcement agency, appointed on or after January 1, 1999, as a condition of continued employment, shall complete the POST training course within two years of appointment. (Ed. Code, § 39672; Pen. Code, § 832.3.)

School Police Reserves

In 1994, the Legislature authorized school districts to establish unpaid volunteer school police reserve officer corps to supplement the school security or police department. (Ed. Code, § 35021.5.) Any person deputized as a school police reserve officer must complete the mandatory training required under existing law. (Pen. Code, §§ 830.6, 832.2.)

School Security Personnel

School security officers are not peace officers, but have the same primary duties. School security patrol jurisdiction is limited to offenses against school personnel, students or property committed on or in the vicinity of school premises, except when officers must go beyond school grounds in connection with school-related offenses. (58 Ops.Cal.Atty.Gen. 363 (1975).)

In 1998, the Legislature and the Governor increased training requirements for school security officers and guards. All security officers and guards employed by a school district for more than 20 hours per week must complete a 24-hour training course developed by the Department of Consumer Affairs' Bureau of Security and Investigative Services.[11] (Bus. & Prof. Code § 7583.45; Ed. Code, § 38001.5.)

Duty to Report

State law imposes duties on school administrators, teachers and other employees to report certain criminal acts to law enforcement officials. They are also mandated to report reasonable suspicions of child abuse to local law enforcement or a child protective agency such as Children's Protective Services (CPS). Administrators do not have the legal authority to withhold this information from law enforcement officials because the safety of a victim or potential victims must be considered. School employees who fail to report

---

[11] Refer to http://www.cde.ca.gov/spbranch/safety/sb162advisory.pdf for a training course advisory on the approved curriculum information.

certain known or suspected crimes are, themselves, in violation of the law. In general, they may be subject to fines, jail or both; they also may lose their license or credential. (Ed. Code, § 44421.) Failure to report child abuse may result in personal civil liability. (*Landeros v. Flood* (1975) 17 Cal.3d 399.) As a reminder, reporting child abuse to school police does not meet the mandatory reporting requirements as school police departments are not considered a "child protective agency." (Pen. Code, § 11165.9.)

Reporting Criminal Acts of Students

It is a criminal offense for teachers or administrators to fail to notify law enforcement if a student commits one of the following specified criminal acts:

Attacking or menacing a school employee. If a student attacks, assaults, physically threatens or menaces a school employee, the employee and his or her supervisor must promptly report the incident to law enforcement. Failure to do so is an infraction and will result in a fine of up to $1,000. (Ed. Code, § 44014, subd. (a).) Filing a report that complies with school district governing board regulations does not relieve the employee or supervisor of the responsibility to notify law enforcement. If any school district governing board member, county superintendent of schools or school district employee directly or indirectly inhibits or impedes the person from making the report, he or she will be guilty of an infraction and may be fined $500 to $1,000. (Ed. Code, § 44014, subd. (c).)

Committing assault with a deadly weapon. If a student commits an assault with a deadly weapon, the principal or principal's designee must notify local law enforcement **before** suspending or expelling the student. (Ed. Code, § 48902, subd. (a).) Furthermore, the principal or principal's designee shall, within one school day after suspension or expulsion of a student, notify the appropriate law enforcement authority or school district of any acts of the student involving possession or sale of narcotics or of a controlled substance or a violation of Penal Code sections 626.9 (Gun-Free School Zone Act) or 626.10. (Ed. Code, § 48902, subd. (b).) Deliberately failing to do so is a misdemeanor and will result in a fine of up to $500. (Ed. Code, § 48902, subd. (e).) Moreover, if the suspended student is not immediately referred to local law enforcement, and he or she injures another student or person, the school may be found liable. A principal, principal's designee or any other person reporting a known or suspected act, cannot be held civilly or criminally liable as a result of reporting the incident unless it can be proven that the report was false. (Ed. Code, § 48902, subd. (d).)

Possessing or selling drugs. If a student possesses or sells narcotics or a controlled substance, the principal or principal's designee shall notify local law enforcement within one school day. (Ed. Code, § 48902, subd. (c).)

Possessing weapons on campus. If a student on campus possesses a firearm, dirk, dagger, ice pick, folding knife with locking blade or knife with blade longer than 2-1/2 inches, razor with unguarded blade, taser or stun gun, spot marker or any instrument that expels a metallic projectile (e.g., a BB or pellet) using air pressure, CO_2 or spring action, the principal must notify law enforcement. (Ed. Code, § 48902; Pen. Code, §§ 626.9, 626.10.)

Reporting criminal acts against children: child abuse. Teachers are often the first people to observe subtle or dramatic changes in student behavior and appearance that may indicate child abuse. Child abuse is defined as a physical injury inflicted by other than accidental means by another person. It also includes sexual abuse, willful cruelty or unjustifiable punishment, unlawful corporal punishment or injury or neglect. Child abuse does not mean a "mutual affray" (i.e., mutual combat) between minors, or injury caused by the use of reasonable, necessary force by peace officers employed or engaged by a public school in order to stop a disturbance. (Pen. Code, §11165.6.)

Mandated reporting of child abuse. Teachers, principals, school administrative officers, child welfare and attendance supervisors, certificated student personnel employees, school child abuse prevention program staff, classified or day camp personnel, school medical or mental health staff and/or child care facility workers are mandated reporters who must report reasonable suspicions of child abuse. Any individual working in one of the job categories listed above who knows or reasonably suspects that a minor (a child under 18 years of age) has been abused at school or elsewhere must immediately report the suspicion by phone, and within 36 hours in writing, to the local police or sheriff's department, county child welfare services agency or county juvenile probation department. (Pen. Code, § 11166.)

Instructional aides, teacher's aides or teaching assistants at any public or private school, and classified employees at any public school, are also required by law to report suspicion of child abuse if they have received training on reporting, and the school district has informed the California Department of Education of the training. Districts that do not train such employees must report the reasons why they have not done so to the California Department of Educa-tion. (Pen. Code, § 11165.7, subds. (b) & (c).) School district police or security departments are mandated to report child abuse, but are not authorized to take child abuse reports. (Pen. Code, § 11165.9.) (For additional information on recognizing and reporting child abuse, see the *Child Abuse Prevention Handbook* and *Child Abuse: Educator's Responsibilities*.)[12]

Failure by a mandated reporter to report child abuse cases is a misdemeanor punishable by a jail sentence of up to six months, a fine of up to $1,000 or both. (Pen. Code, § 11172, subd. (e).) Educators who fail to report may also risk losing their license or credential. The California Commission on Teacher Credentialing can privately admonish, revoke or suspend a credential because of immoral or unprofessional conduct, or if any individual persistently defies or refuses to obey the laws regulating service in California public schools. (Ed. Code, § 44421.) Moreover, a failure to report

---

[12] Office of the Attorney General, Crime and Violence Prevention Center, P.O. Box 944255, Sacramento, CA 94244-2550.

may result in personal civil liability. (*Landeros v. Flood, supra*, 17 Cal.3d at p. 399.)

Court decisions have held that the Child Abuse and Neglect Reporting Act discussed above provides an absolute immunity from subsequent liability by mandated reporters "for acts committed in a professional capacity or within the scope of employment giving rise to the obligation to report as well as for the act of reporting." (*Spitler v. Children's Institute International* (1992) 11 Cal.App.4th 432, 440.)

Child Abuse by School Personnel

In *John R. v. Oakland Unified School District*, a 14-year-old junior high student was allegedly sexually molested by a teacher during an off-campus tutoring session. The California Supreme Court rejected the theory that the exercise of job-created authority of teachers over students made the district liable. As a matter of public policy, the court found that school districts should not be held vicariously liable for torts resulting from employee molestation of students. However, a district may be liable if its own direct negligence is established. (*John R. v. Oakland Unified School District* (1989) 48 Cal.3d 438.)

Kimberly M. v. Los Angeles Unified School District, which was decided after being returned by the California Supreme Court to the lower appellate court for reconsideration, follows the rationale of John R., even though the child involved was only five years old, and the molestation occurred at school. (*Kimberly M. v. Los Angeles Unified School District* (1989) 215 Cal.App.3d 545.)

However, students molested by teachers may pursue a remedy in federal court. Schools may be found liable for violating student federal civil rights if the schools do not protect students from reasonably foreseeable sexual assaults by teachers. (42 U.S.C. § 1983; *Stoneking v. Bradford Area School District* (3d Cir.1989) 882 F.2d 720.)

Upon request, the school district governing board or county education office must make available guidelines for filing child abuse
complaints against a school employee, as specified in Education
Code section 33308.1, to a minor student's parents or guardians in
their primary language. When verbally communicating these procedures to a parent or guardian whose primary language is not English,
the governing board must provide interpretive services. (Ed. Code,
§ 48987.)

Sex Crimes Against Children: Prosecution

Sex crimes committed against children must be prosecuted within
either three years or six years of the date of the crime, depending
on the age of the victim. (Pen. Code, §§ 800, 801.) There are,
however, two statutory exceptions.

Penal Code section 803, subdivision (f), extends the normally-
applicable statute of limitations in child sexual abuse cases if all the
following conditions are met:

- The complaint is filed within one year of a report to a responsible adult or agency, meaning a person required to
  report child abuse pursuant to the Child Abuse and Neglect
  Reporting Act, such as a child care custodian, health practi-
  tioner, or employee of a child protective agency. (Pen. Code
  § 11166.)
- By a child under the age of 18 years that she was a
  victim of a specified sex offense; and the defendant has
  committed at least one specified sex offense against the
  same victim within the normally-applicable statute of limitation.

Example: The defendant fondled his niece when she visited him
in 1991, 1993 and 1996. She reported the crimes to her teacher
in 2000, when she was 17. By that time, the generally-applicable
six-year statute of limitations for the first two crimes had expired.
However, because it had not expired for the third crime, the uncle
may be charged with all three crimes if the charges are filed within
one year of the date the victim reported them to her teacher.

Penal Code section 803, subdivision (g), extends the normally-applicable statute of limitations in child sexual abuse cases if all the following conditions are met:

- The complaint is filed within one year of the date a person of any age reports to a law enforcement agency that he or she was a victim of a specified sex offense.
- The crime involved substantial sexual conduct there is independent, admissible evidence that clearly and convincingly corroborates the victim's allegation.

Example: The defendant had sexual intercourse with his daughter in 1980. She reported the crime to the police in 2000. By that time, the generally-applicable six-year statute of limitations had expired. However, if there is independent corroboration of the crime, the father may be charged with the crime if the charges are filed within one year of the date the victim reported it to the police.

Sex Crimes Against Children: Civil Claims

Previously, the statute of limitations for filing a civil claim against a third party who had a duty to protect a victim from childhood sexual abuse was one year from the date on which the victim reached the age of majority, or 19 years old. (Code of Civ. Proc., § 340.1.)

Effective January 1, 1999, the statute of limitations for filing against these third parties was extended until the victim turned 26 years of age. (Statutes of 1998, Chapter 1032, AB 1651 (Ortiz).)

Because the 1999 law contained no statement of retroactivity, however, in a case in which the victim was 19 years of age as of January 1, 1999, the cause of action was time barred. Thus, effective January 1, 2000, the law was amended again to make the new statutes of limitations for childhood sexual abuse cases against third parties retroactive, so that victims between the ages of 19 and 26 years may bring a cause of action against third parties, unless there was a final adjudication prior to January 1, 1999. (Statutes of 1999, Chapter 120, SB 674 (Ortiz).)

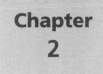
School Attendance

When educators work together with law enforcement and probation officers to enforce compulsory education laws, these partnerships provide an excellent means of preventing truancy and delinquency. Truancy prevention strategies require close cooperation between schools and probation departments, district attorneys' offices and juvenile courts as well as students, their parents or guardians and members of the community.

This chapter highlights how the laws concerning compulsory education and truancy are enforced by school officials, school attendance review boards (SARBs), district attorneys, law enforcement, probation officers and juvenile courts. It also describes truancy prevention strategies authorized by California law.

Laws Governing Attendance

Compulsory Education

Full-time school attendance is compulsory for California children between the ages of 6 and 18. Most students meet their full-time attendance requirements in a comprehensive school or through continuation education. (Ed. Code, § 48400.) Except under certain circumstances, the legal age for leaving school is 18. Education Code section 48410 exempts high school graduates, Regional Occupational Program (ROP) students, private school students, students with dependents and others as specified in the section. Youth who are 16 years or older, but under age 18, are minimally required to attend continuation education classes or regional occupational center programs. Employed youth are permitted to attend a minimum program schedule. Youth who are 16 years or older, or who have completed the 10th grade, may be exempted from compulsory attendance by passing the California High School Proficiency Examination and receiving parental permission. (Ed. Code, §§ 48200, 48400, 48412.) A child who is between the ages of 16 and 18, when a leave of absence is requested, may be granted such a leave from compulsory continuation education classes for up to two semesters, if the following three conditions are satisfied:

- The governing board has adopted a written policy to allow student leaves of absence.
- The leave purpose is supervised travel, study, training or work not available to the student under another education program.
- A written agreement is entered into which is signed by the child, the child's parent or guardian, the school administrator and the classroom teacher. (Ed. Code, § 48416.)

Truancy

A truant is "any pupil subject to compulsory full-time education or to compulsory continuation education who is absent from school without valid excuse three full days in one school year or tardy or absent for more than any 30-minute period during the school day without a valid excuse on three occasions in one school year, or any combination thereof. . . . " (Ed. Code, § 48260, subd. (a).) Truants will be reported to the attendance supervisor or to the school district superintendent. *(Ibid.)*

A student who has been reported as a truant "who is again absent from school without valid excuse one or more days, or tardy on one or more days, will again be reported as a truant to the attendance supervisor or the superintendent of the district." (Ed. Code, § 48261.)

A student who has been reported as a truant three or more times in one school year will be considered a habitual truant if an appropriate district employee has tried to hold at least one conference with the student and his or her parent or guardian, after reporting the situation to the attendance supervisor or school district superintendent. (Ed. Code, §§ 48260, 48262.)

Taking a Truant Into Custody

Students who are not in school during school hours (i.e., truants) may be arrested and taken into custody. The California Supreme Court held that law enforcement had reasonable suspicion to detain and question a youth to determine whether he was truant, based on his "youthful appearance." The court found that the public's interest in enforcing compulsory education laws and the propriety of a truancy arrest under Education Code section 48264 outweighed the slight interference with personal liberty caused by the detention. (*In re James D.* (1987) 43 Cal.3d 903.) According to Education Code section 48264, the following individuals are authorized to arrest or assume temporary custody of any minor subject to compulsory education found away from his or her home and absent from school without a valid excuse within the county, city or school district:

- An attendance supervisor (or supervisor's designee).
- A peace officer.
- A school administrator (or administrator's designee).
- A probation officer.

Any person arresting or assuming temporary custody of a truant is required immediately to deliver the minor to one of the following:

- The parent, guardian or other person having charge of the minor.
- The school from which the minor is absent.
- A school or district designated, non-secure youth service or community center, for counseling before returning the minor home or to school.
- A school counselor or student services and attendance officer at a police station, for immediate counseling before the minor returns or is returned home or to school.
- The probation officer of the county having jurisdiction, if the minor is found to be a habitual truant. (Ed. Code, § 48265.)

An individual who arrests or assumes temporary custody of a truant is required to report the incident and the arrangements made for the minor to school authorities of the city, or city and county, or school district, and to the minor's parent or guardian. (Ed. Code, § 48266.)

Various municipalities have enacted truancy prevention ordinances. One such municipality is the city of Rialto, whose ordinance became effective September 1, 1995. This ordinance forbids any minor to loiter, idle, wander, stroll or play in or upon public streets, highways, roads, alleys, parks, playgrounds, parking areas, or other public grounds, public places, places of amusement and eating places, vacant lots or other unimproved places, or any place open to the public between the hours of 7:30 a.m. and 2:30 p.m. on the days when said minor's school is in session. Students violating this ordinance are subject to a fine not to exceed $250 and/or required to perform community service. Parents, guardians or other adult persons having care and custody of a minor who permit the student to violate this ordinance are subject to a fine not to exceed $1,000 and/or are required to perform community service.

Consequences of Being a Truant

Any minor who is a truant under Education Code section 48260 is subject to the following:

- If the student is truant for the first time, a peace officer may personally issue the offender a written warning. A record of the warning may be retained by the school and the officer's law enforcement agency. (Ed. Code, § 48264.5, subd. (a).)
- After a second truancy in the same school year, the student may be assigned by the school to an after-school or weekend study program. (Ed. Code, § 48264.5, subd. (b).)
- If the student fails to successfully complete the assigned study program or is truant for a third time, he or she may be required to attend a SARB or truancy mediation program. (Note: SARBs are discussed in greater detail later in this chapter under "School District Referrals.") If the district does not have such a program, the student may have to attend a comparable program elsewhere, provided that it is approved by the district's attendance supervisor. (Ed. Code, § 48264.5, subds. (b) & (c).)

If the student does not complete the truancy mediation program or is a truant for the fourth time in the same school year, he or she "shall be classified as a habitual truant . . . and will be within the jurisdiction of the juvenile court, which may then adjudge [order] the pupil to be a ward of the court under Section 601 of the Welfare and Institutions Code." (Ed. Code, § 48264.5, subd. (d).)

School District Responses to Truancy

Notifying Parents or Guardians of Student Truant Status

When a student is initially classified as a truant, the school district must notify his or her parent or guardian by first-class mail or other reasonable means. In addition, the notification must include the following information:

- The parent or guardian is obligated to ensure that the student attends school.
- Parents or guardians who fail to meet this obligation may be guilty of an infraction and subject to prosecution.
- The student may be subject to prosecution under Education Code section 48264, as discussed above. He or she may also be subject to suspension, restriction or delay of his or her driving privilege under Vehicle Code section 13202.7.
- The parent or guardian has the right to meet and discuss the truancy situation and possible solutions with appropriate school personnel.
- School officials may recommend that the parent or guardian accompany the student to school and attend classes with him or her for one day.
- There are alternative educational programs for the student in the district. (Ed. Code, § 48260.5.)

Alternatives to Suspension or Expulsion

The Legislature intended that schools employ alternatives to suspension or expulsion when students are truant, tardy or other-wise absent from school. (Ed. Code, §§ 48900, 489005.) When state law does not require suspension or expulsion, a student may be subject to one of the following alternatives, if authorized by local rules:

Detention. A student may be detained for up to one hour after school for disciplinary or other reasons unless he or she must wait longer than that for a school bus. (Title 5, Cal. Code Regs., §§ 307, 353.)

Recess restriction. A teacher may restrict the time a student is allowed for recess for disciplinary purposes. (Ed. Code, § 44807.5.)

In-house suspension. Schools may establish in-house suspension as an alternative if a student "poses no imminent danger or threat" to the school, other students or staff, or if an action to expel the student has not been initiated. Students under in-house suspension will be kept apart from other children at the school in a separate classroom, building or site. (Ed. Code, § 48911.1.)

Weekend classes. Schools may also schedule classes on Saturday or Sunday, or both, for unexcused absences that occur during the week. (Ed. Code, § 37223.)

Community service on school grounds during non-school hours. Principals or their designees may assign students community service instead of using disciplinary measures. Such service may include work performed on school grounds, including outdoor beautification, campus improvements and teacher or peer assistance programs. (Ed. Code, § 48900.6.)

Opportunity school, class or program. A student may be assigned to an opportunity school, class or program designed for youngsters who are or are at risk of becoming habitually truant from school, irregular in attendance or insubordinate or disorderly while at school. Students who are habitually truant, do not attend regularly, or display insubordinate or disorderly behavior at such a school, class or program must be referred by the attendance supervisor or other school board designee to a SARB. (Ed. Code, §§ 48630 *et seq.*)

Community schools. A community school may be established and maintained by any county board of education to enroll students who: 1) have been expelled from school while attending either continuation classes, opportunity classes or alternative classes; 2) are referred by a district (because of a SARB hearing or at the request of a parent or guardian); 3) are probation-referred dependents or wards of the court, or are on probation or parole and not attending any school; or 4) are homeless. (Ed. Code, §§ 1980 *et seq.*)

Each student's educational program must be individually assessed and prescribed. The community school course of study will be adopted by the county board of education and must enable students to continue academic work leading to the completion of a regular high school program. (Ed. Code, § 1983.) Students who have been expelled for possession of a firearm at school or at an off-campus school activity may be enrolled in community school. (Ed. Code, § 48915.2.)

Community day schools. A school district governing board may establish one or more community day schools for students in kindergarten or grades 1-12 who meet one or both of the following conditions: 1) they have been expelled for any reason; 2) they are probation-referred according to Welfare and Institutions Code sections 300 or 602 by a SARB (or other district-level referral process if the district does not operate a SARB). (Ed. Code, §§ 48660-48664.) If students expelled for one or more serious or mandatory offenses listed under Education Code section 48915, subdivisions (b) and (d) are served, the program cannot be offered at a comprehensive school site unless the county superintendent of schools certifies that no alternative study program is available at a different location.[13]

---

[13] See *Expulsion Policies and Educational Placements Program Advisory,* SPB: 95/96-04. Sacramento: California Department of Education, 1995.

School District Referrals

School districts may refer minor students to a SARB or probation department (if the latter has elected to accept referrals) when students are habitually truant, irregular in school attendance, habitually insubordinate or disorderly during school attendance.

School Attendance Review Boards

SARBs were created in 1977 to help schools provide "intensive guidance and coordinated community services" for students with school attendance or behavior problems. (Ed. Code, § 48320, subd. (a).) SARBs also hear cases concerning students from opportunity schools, classes or programs. (Ed. Code, § 48638.)

Local and county level SARBs include representatives from the county superintendent of schools, school district and probation, welfare, law enforcement and youth-serving agencies; parents; and school guidance, child welfare and school attendance personnel. (Ed. Code, § 48321, subd. (a).) SARB members meet regularly and work collaboratively to assess the specific circumstances of each student referred to them.[14]

The attendance supervisor or other board-designated person referring a student to a SARB must provide the name and address of the SARB or probation department and the reason for the referral in writing to the minor and his or her parent or guardian. The notice will inform the minor and parent or guardian that they must meet with the person making the referral and the SARB or probation officer to consider what actions will be taken as a consequence of the referral. (Ed. Code, § 48263.)

The SARB or probation officer may determine that community services are available that may resolve a student's behavior or

---

[14] See *SARB Operations: Operations and Resources, Handbook for School Attendance Review Boards,* Sacramento: California Department of Education, 1995.

attendance problems. Under these circumstances, the SARB or probation officer will instruct the student or his or her parent or guardian, or both, to utilize those services. Proof of compliance with this directive may be required. (Ed. Code, § 48263.)

Any SARB may direct a school district to file a criminal complaint against the parent or guardian (or other person in charge of the minor) for failure to respond to the directives of the SARB or to services offered for the child. (Ed. Code, § 48291; Welf. & Inst. Code, § 601.2.) Unless excused or exempted, the parent, guardian or other person in charge of the minor will be subjected to fines and/ or ordered to attend parent education and counseling programs for subsequent violations. (Ed. Code, § 48293.)

If a minor fails to respond to SARB directives or to services, the SARB may refer the minor to the probation department or county welfare department. (Ed. Code, § 48263; Welf. & Inst. Code, §§ 601, subd. (b), 601.2, 601.4.)

The SARB or probation department may also determine that available public and private services cannot correct school attendance or behavior problems. If so, the SARB or probation department may: 1) propose using alternative solutions to the juvenile court system; 2) make maximum use of appropriate community and regional resources before turning to the judicial system; or 3) promote the idea that using a community resource alternative requires a commitment by citizens and agencies to continually improve this type of alternative and to create such resources where none are available. (Ed. Code, § 48320, subd. (b).)

Truancy Mediation Programs

If existing community services cannot resolve a student's truant or insubordinate behavior, or if the student or the parents or guardians (or both) fail to respond to SARB or probation department directives or to services provided, the SARB may contact the local district attorney's truancy mediation program. (Ed. Code, §§ 48263, 48263.5.)

Truancy mediation programs are the final step with the student and family before prosecuting the student for failing to comply with the compulsory education requirements. The district attorney or probation officer may notify the truant's parents or guardians that they may be prosecuted for failing to have their minor attend school. If the school district informs the district attorney or probation officer, or both, that the child continues to be classified as truant after this notification, either official may request a meeting with the parents or guardians and the child under Welfare and Institutions Code section 601.3 to discuss the possible legal consequences of the minor's truancy. (Ed. Code, § 48260.6, subd. (c) & (d).)

Notification of the meeting must be provided to each person required to attend at least five days before, either personally or by certified mail with return receipt requested. It must contain the following information:

- Name and address of the person to whom the notice is directed.
- Date, time and place of the meeting.
- Name of the minor classified as the truant.
- Legal code section under which the meeting is being requested.

The notice must also inform the recipient that the district attorney may file a criminal complaint against the parents or guardians under Education Code section 48293, should they fail to ensure that their child attends school. (Welf. & Inst. Code, § 601.3.)

When the meeting begins, the district attorney or probation officer must advise the parents or guardians and the child that any statements they make can be used against them in subsequent court proceedings. After the meeting, the probation officer or district attorney may file a petition under Welfare and Institutions Code section 601 if it is determined that available community resources cannot resolve the truancy problem, or if the student or his or her parents or guardians, or both, have failed to respond to services provided or to the instructions of the school, SARB, probation officer or district attorney.

After attending a SARB or truancy mediation program, or a program operated by a probation department acting as a SARB, a student who is again truant is subject to suspension or revocation of all driving privileges; his or her license must be surrendered. If the minor does not yet have a license, his or her right to obtain one may be postponed for one year. For each additional truancy incident, the court can add to the waiting time for driving privileges. (Ed. Code, § 48264.5, subd. (d); Veh. Code, § 13202.7.)

If the district attorney or probation department has not chosen to participate in the truancy mediation program described in Education Code section 48260.6, the SARB or probation officer may direct the county superintendent of schools to request a petition for the student in the county juvenile court. When the petition is presented, the juvenile court will hear all evidence relating to the request. The SARB or the probation officer must submit a report to the juvenile court documenting efforts to secure attendance, along with recommendations as to what action the court should take regarding the case. (Ed. Code, § 48263.)

In counties having no SARB, the district attorney or probation officer is authorized to establish a truancy mediation program. However, they are required to coordinate their efforts in deciding which county office can most effectively operate a local truancy mediation program. (Welf. & Inst. Code, § 601.3, subd. (f).)

Truancy Court

Truancy courts are scattered throughout the state. Most referrals to truancy court are made through the SARB process and these courts meet once a month with the family in a formal setting to discuss the child's truancy and possible consequences if the behavior continues. A truancy court is generally comprised of a judge, bailiff, probation officer, school representative and police officer. All members are volunteers. If a minor or parent fails to comply with the orders of the truancy court, the district attorney is legally able to pursue prosecution. If a school does not have an affiliated truancy court, families are referred by the SARB to the district attorney's mediation program.

Juvenile Court

If the SARB determines that available community services cannot resolve the truancy or insubordination problems of a student, it must direct the county superintendent of schools to request a petition on the student's behalf in the county juvenile court. If the court sustains the petition, it may render any appropriate judgement, including requiring the parent or guardian to bring the youngster to the opportunity school, class or program at the beginning of each school day, for the remainder of the school year. (Ed. Code, § 48638.)

Jurisdiction Over Habitually Disobedient or Truant Minors

The juvenile court has jurisdiction over a minor and may adjudge (order) him or her as a ward of the court if he or she is under age 18 and:

- Persistently or habitually refuses to obey the "reasonable and proper orders or directions" of his or her parents or guardians, or is beyond the control of these individuals.
- Violates any city or county curfew based solely on age.
- Has four or more truancies within one school year.
- Receives a SARB or probation officer determination that available public and private services cannot correct the minor's habitual truancy or "persistent or habitual refusal to obey the reasonable and proper orders or directions of school authorities."
- Fails to respond to the instructions of a SARB or probation officer or to services provided. (Welf. & Inst. Code, § 601.)

The Legislature did not intend for minors, who are adjudged wards of the court for any of these reasons, to be removed from the custody of their parents or guardians except during school hours. To the extent possible, a minor who is adjudged a ward under one of the conditions listed above will not be permitted to have contact with any student ordered to participate in a truancy program or equivalent program. (Welf. & Inst. Code, § 602.) In addition, "any

38

person who is under the age of 18 years when he violates any law ... other than an ordinance based solely on age, is within the jurisdiction of the juvenile court, which may adjudge such person to be a ward of the court." (*Ibid.*)

Habitually truant students who are adjudged wards of the court will be required to do one or more of the following:

- Perform court-approved community service through a public or private non-profit agency for at least 20, but no more than 40, hours within a 90-day period during a time other than school hours or hours of employment. If the student fails to complete the assigned community service, the probation officer must report this to the court.
- Pay a fine not to exceed $100, for which the parent or guardian may be jointly liable.
- Attend a court-approved truancy prevention program.

Once a student is declared a ward of the court and required to attend school, any truancy, tardiness or insubordination must be reported by school staff to the court and probation officer within ten days of the violation. (Ed. Code, § 48267.) The probation department and the district attorney's office may file a petition to bring the matter before a judge to request sanctions. (Welf. & Inst. Code, § 777.) In 1998, the California Supreme Court held that because of its contempt power, the juvenile court was authorized to order the confinement during non-school hours of a minor who had been made a ward of the court and was later found in contempt of court for willfully disobeying a court order to attend school. (*In re Michael G.* (1988) 44 Cal.3d 283.)

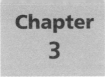

Chapter
3

Disciplining Students

California law gives educators the responsibility to maintain a moral, educational and disciplined school environment. To accomplish this charge, school districts and their schools are authorized to establish disciplinary policies and procedures, and school employees have the duty to enforce them. (Ed. Code, § 35291.5.) When school rules are violated, there must be consequences; students must be held accountable for their actions. And in order to have safe, secure and peaceful schools, order must be maintained. Schools must provide students, staff, parents and guardians with clear and concise information about school rules, and school officials must effectively and consistently implement these rules.

This chapter presents an overview of laws pertaining to student discipline. This publication does not address federal and state laws pertaining to the discipline of special education students.[15]

Development of Local Rules

California law requires each school district governing board to set reasonable rules governing discipline in the schools under its jurisdiction. (Ed. Code, §§ 35010, 35291.) These rules and regulations should be clear and concise and must include the procedures for expulsion hearings. The law further specifies that each school must adopt disciplinary rules and procedures every four years. (Ed. Code, § 35291.5.) These rules must be developed with input from students, teachers, parents, security and community members and adopted by a school panel on which the principal and teachers are

---

[15] For information on laws pertaining to Special Education and pertinent Legal Advisories, contact the California Department of Education, Special Education Division at (916) 445-4613.

represented. (Ed. Code, § 35291.5, subd. (a).) Students who willfully defy school district rules may be suspended or expelled. (Ed. Code, § 48900.)

Skateboards/rollerblades. A local authority may adopt rules and regulations by ordinance or resolution prohibiting or restricting a person from riding or propelling skateboards/Rollerblades on highways, sidewalks or roadways. (Vehicle Code, § 21967.)

Electronic Signaling Devices

No school shall permit the possession or use of any electronic signaling device that operates through the transmission or receipt of radio waves, including, but not limited to, paging and signaling equipment, by students of the school while the students are on campus, attending school-sponsored activities, or under the supervision and control of school district employees, without the prior consent of the principal or principal's designee. (Ed. Code, § 48901.5.)

Notice to Parents/Guardians and Students

At the beginning of each school year, or at the time of initial enrollment for transfers, schools are required to inform students and their parents or guardians in writing of the local rules and disciplinary policies and file a copy of these rules with the district superintendent. (Ed. Code, §§ 35291.5, subds. (b) & (c).) When new grounds for student discipline are added to state law, governing boards and schools must add them to their district procedures and inform students and their parents or guardians of these rule changes before using them as the basis for disciplinary actions.

Limitations

School discipline policies may not impose sanctions that would discourage the exercise of rights guaranteed under the U.S. Constitution or state Constitution. The limits of these rights will be examined in the next chapter.

Corporal Punishment

Schools may consider the use of sanctions against students when school disciplinary policies are violated. However, all forms of corporal punishment are prohibited. Corporal punishment means the willful infliction of physical pain on a student. The use of reasonable and necessary force by a school employee to stop a disturbance threatening physical injury to people or property damage, for purposes of self-defense or to obtain weapons or other dangerous objects controlled by a student is not considered corporal punishment. Physical pain or discomfort resulting from athletic competition or other such recreational activity in which students voluntarily participate is also not corporal punishment. (Ed. Code, §§ 49000, 49001.) An individual teacher or school official who violates the Education Code and administers corporal punishment to a student may face substantial personal civil liability for his or her actions.

Grounds for Student Discipline

Activities Warranting Suspension or Expulsion

Grounds for suspension and expulsion are specified in Education Code section 48900. A student may be suspended from school or recommended for expulsion if the principal or district superintendent determines that the enrolled student has engaged in any of the following acts described below:

Physical injury. Threatening or causing physical injury to another person or attempting to do so, or willfully using force or violence except in self-defense. (Ed. Code, §§ 48900, subd. (a), 48915, subd. (a)(1); 48915.2.)

Robbery or extortion. Taking part in robbery or extortion, or attempting either. (Ed. Code, §§ 48900, subd. (e), 48915, subd. (a)(4), 48915.2.)

Dangerous weapons. Possessing, selling, using or supplying any firearm, knife, explosive or other dangerous object, unless written

43

permission is obtained from a certificated school employee and approved by the principal or principal's designee. (Ed. Code, §§ 48900, subd. (b); 48915, subd. (a)(2); 48915.2.)

Imitation firearm. Possessing a replica of a firearm that is so substantially similar in physical properties to an existing firearm as to lead a reasonable person to conclude that the replica is a firearm. (Ed. Code, § 48900, subd. (m).)

Alcohol and drugs. Unlawfully possessing, using, selling, supplying or being under the influence of any alcoholic beverage, intoxicant or controlled substance. (Ed. Code, §§ 48900, subd. (c); 48915, subd. (a)(3); 48915.2.) Selling substances represented to be alcohol, drugs or other intoxicants. (Ed. Code, § 48900, subd. (d).)

Paraphernalia. Offering, arranging or negotiating to sell any drug paraphernalia, as defined in Health and Safety Code section 11014.5. (Ed. Code, § 48900, subd. (j).)

Smoking. Possessing or using tobacco, or any products containing tobacco or nicotine, on campus or at school-sponsored activities. (Ed. Code, §§ 48900, subd. (h); 48901.) School districts are required to take "all practical steps" to discourage high school students from smoking. (Ed. Code, § 48901, subd. (b).)

Damaging school or private property. Causing or attempting to cause damage to school or private property. (Ed. Code, § 48900, subd. (f).) This includes defacing or destroying such property. A student's refusal to return school property loaned to him or her would also constitute an offense. (5 Cal. Code of Regs., § 305.)

Stealing school or private property. Stealing or attempting to steal school or private property, or knowingly receiving stolen property. (Ed. Code, § 48900, subds. (g) & (l).)

Profanity and obscenity. Committing an obscene act or engaging in habitual profanity or vulgarity. (Ed. Code, § 48900, subd. (i).) An isolated act of profanity or vulgarity is generally not sufficient grounds for suspension or expulsion under this code section. Lesser penalties, however, may be used for isolated use of lewd and vulgar speech. Society has an interest in teaching students the boundaries of socially appropriate behavior. This interest is served by restricting obscene speech while protecting expressions of political views — even unpopular and controversial ones.

Disruption or defiance. Disrupting school activities or otherwise willfully defying the valid authority of supervisors, teachers, administrators or other school personnel performing their duties. (Ed. Code, § 48900, subd. (k).)

This subdivision is significant not only for its general applicability, but also because it can be used to enforce the reasonable rules and regulations of individual school districts. One important limit to this provision is that a student may not be disciplined for politely disobeying an order that would violate his or her constitutional or statutory rights (e.g., for refusing to stand up and salute the flag, no matter how often the student refuses). The courts have repeatedly held that students have a constitutional right to refuse to stand and salute the flag and may not be punished for exercising this right.

Sexual harassment. Making "unwelcome sexual advances, requests for sexual favors, and other verbal, visual, or physical conduct of a sexual nature. . . . " (Ed. Code, § 212.5.) Sexual harassment, as defined above, is grounds for suspension or expulsion for students enrolled in grades 4-12. The alleged conduct "must be considered by a reasonable person of the same gender as the victim to be sufficiently severe or pervasive to have a negative impact upon the individual's academic performance or to create an intimidating, hostile, or offensive educational environment." (Ed. Code, § 48900.2.) A copy of the district's sexual harassment policy must be made available to parents and guardians of students at the beginning of the school year or upon enrollment. (Ed. Code, § 212.6.)

Sexual assault. Committing or attempting to commit an act as listed in Penal Code sections 261, 266 (c), 286, 288, 288 (a) or 289, or committing a sexual battery as defined in Penal Code section 243.4. (Ed. Code, § 48900, subd. (n).)

Intimidating a student witness. Harassing, threatening or intimidating a student who is a complaining witness or witness in a school disciplinary proceeding for the purpose of either preventing the student from acting as a witness or retaliating against him or her for being a witness, or both. (Ed. Code, § 48900, subd. (o).)

Hate violence. Causing, attempting to cause, threatening to cause or participating in an act of hate violence may be subject to suspension or expulsion. Hate violence, defined as any act punishable under Penal Code sections 422.6, 422.7 and 422.75, is a specific crime that is committed because of the victim's race, color, religion, ancestry, national origin, disability, gender or sexual orientation or because the defendant perceives that the victim has one or more of those characteristics. (Ed. Code, § 48900.3; Pen. Code, §§ 422.6, 422.7, 422.75, 11410-11414.)

Any person who burns, desecrates or destroys a cross or other religious symbol, knowing it to be a religious symbol, on the property of a primary school, junior high school or high school for the purpose of terrorizing any person who attends or works at the school or who is otherwise associated with the school, shall be punished by imprisonment in state prison or county jail. (Pen. Code, §§ 11410 - 11414.)

The Alameda County Office of Education and the California Department of Education jointly developed a school-based resource guide designed specifically for schools throughout the state to address hate-motivated behavior in schools.[16]

Harassment. Intentionally harassing, threatening or intimidating another student or group of students severely or pervasively enough

---

[16] *Hate-Motivated Behavior in Schools, Response Strategies for School Boards, Administrators, Law Enforcement and Communities,* Alameda County Office of Education, 313 West Winton Avenue, Hayward, CA 94544; (510) 670-4161.

to disrupt classwork, cause substantial disorder, or threaten student rights by "creating an intimidating or hostile educational environment." (Ed. Code, § 48900.4.)

Terroristic threats. Making terrorist threats against school officials or school property, or both. A terrorist threat is defined as "any statement, whether written or oral, by a person who willfully threatens to commit a crime which will result in death, great bodily injury to another person, or property damage in excess of $1,000, with the specific intent that the statement is to be taken as a threat, even if there is no intent of actually carrying it out, which, on its face and under the circumstances in which it is made, is so unequivocal, unconditional, immediate, and specific as to convey to the person threatened, a gravity of purpose and an immediate prospect of execution of the threat, and thereby causes that person reasonably to be in sustained fear for his or her own safety or for his or her own immediate family's safety, or for the protection of school district property, or the personal property of the person threatened or his or her immediate family." (Ed. Code, § 48900.7.)

No student can be suspended or expelled for any of the acts listed above unless these actions are related to a school activity or attendance at school. Suspension or expulsion can occur at any time, including, but not limited to: 1) while a student is on school grounds; 2) while he or she is going to or coming from school; 3) during the lunch period, whether on or off campus; 4) during or while a student is going to or coming from a school-sponsored activity. (Ed. Code, § 48900.)

School District's Duty to Inform Teachers

School districts are required to inform teachers about any student who engages in or is reasonably suspected to have committed any of the acts described above, except those related to the possession or use of tobacco or any products containing tobacco or nicotine. An officer or employee who knowingly fails to provide information about a student who has engaged in, or who is reasonably suspected to have engaged in, the acts referred to in section 48900, except subdivision (h), is guilty of a misdemeanor, which is punishable by confinement in the county jail for a period not to exceed six months, or by a fine not to exceed $1,000, or both. For the 1996-97 school year and each school year thereafter, the information provided shall be from the previous three school years. (Ed. Code, §§ 48900, 49079.)

Withholding Grades, Transcripts and Diplomas

As long as due process rights are respected, a public or private school may withhold the grades, transcripts or diploma of a student who is responsible for the loss of or damage to personal or school property until his or her parent or guardian has paid for the damages. As noted, rules and regulations should be adopted by the school district governing board before implementing these disciplinary options. (Ed. Code, §§ 48904, 48904.3.)

Before withholding grades, transcripts or diplomas, the school district must notify the student's parent or guardian of the alleged misconduct in writing. When the minor and parent or guardian are unable to pay for the damages or return the property, the school district or private school must provide a program of voluntary work for the minor in lieu of requiring payment of monetary damages. After the volunteer work is completed, the grades, transcripts and diploma of the student must be released.

If a district has decided to withhold a student's grades, transcripts or diploma and receives notification that the student has transferred to another school district in this state, district personnel must notify his or her parent or guardian in writing that its decision to withhold the information will be enforced. Under Education Code section 49068, school districts are required to transfer a student's records to another district when the student transfers to that district. According to the law, a school district may not delay sending student records to another district because the student has willfully damaged school district property, owes the district money for class material or has failed to return a book. (64 Ops.Cal.Atty.Gen. 867 (1981).)

When the school district to which the student has transferred receives notice that the student's former district has withheld his or her grades, transcripts or diploma in accordance with Education Code section 48904, the new school district must also withhold this information until it receives further notice from the district initiating the action that the student's grades, transcripts or diploma can be released. (Ed. Code, § 48904.3.)

Suspension

The Education Code defines suspension as "removal of a pupil from ongoing instruction for adjustment purposes." (Ed. Code, § 48925, subd. (d).) Suspension, like expulsion, should be used when other punishments fail. It may be imposed by a teacher, principal or designee, school superintendent or governing board.

The law requires immediate suspension for possession, selling or otherwise furnishing of firearms. It also allows suspension for a first offense without considering other means of correction if the offense involves physical injuries, dangerous objects or other weapons, unlawful sale of controlled substances, robbery or extortion, or if "the pupil's presence causes a danger to [other] persons . . . or threatens to disrupt the instructional process." (Ed. Code, §§ 48915, subds. (a), (b) & (c); 48900.5.)

Suspension does not occur when a student is: (1) reassigned to another class or program at the same school to receive instruction each day for the amount of time approved by the governing board for his or her grade level; (2) referred to a certificated employee designated by the principal to advise students; (3) removed from class for the remainder of the class period, but not reassigned to another class or program or sent to the principal or principal's designee.

A student cannot be removed from a particular class more than once every five school days. (Ed. Code, § 48925, subd. (d).) Generally, a student may be suspended from school for no more than five consecutive school days and for no more than 20 days in one school year unless for purposes of adjustment, a student enrolls in or transfers to another regular school, an opportunity school or class or a continuation education school or class. In such cases, the total number of school days for which the student may be suspended must not exceed 30 days in any school year. (Ed. Code, §§ 48903, 48911, subd. (a).) A teacher may require a student on suspension to make up any missed assignments or tests. (Ed. Code, § 48913.)

When a student is suspended, a school employee must make a reasonable effort to contact the parents or guardians in person or by telephone, and they must also be notified in writing. (Ed. Code, § 48911, subd. (d).) The school board or district superintendent must also be informed. (Ed. Code, § 48911, subd. (e).) Each school district may establish a policy permitting school officials to meet with the parent or guardian of a suspended student to discuss the cause, duration, relevant school policy and other matters pertaining to the suspension. Parents or guardians are required to "respond without delay" to any request from school officials to attend a conference regarding their child's behavior. However, no penalties may be imposed on the student if the parents or guardians fail to attend the conference. Likewise, reinstatement of the suspended student will not depend on their attendance. (Ed. Code, §§ 48911, subd. (f); 48914.)

Suspensions may be extended by the superintendent or super-intendent's designee if the governing board already is considering expulsion from any school (or suspension for the balance of the semester from a continuation school). A suspension may only be extended until the date the governing board makes a decision about the expulsion. (Ed. Code, §§ 48911, subd. (g); 48912.5.) When a student enrolls or transfers to another regular school, opportunity school or class, or continuation school or class, the 20-day limitation may be extended to 30 days. (Ed. Code, § 48903.)

An extension may be granted only if the school district superinten-dent or superintendent's designee determines that the student's presence at school or in an alternative school would cause a danger to people or property, or threaten to disrupt the instructional process. This determination will be made after holding a meeting to which the student and his or her parents or guardians are invited.

A parent or guardian may request a meeting to challenge and discuss the original suspension. Any meeting to discuss an extension of the expulsion may be held in conjunction with this initial meeting. (Ed. Code, §§ 48914, 48911, subd. (g).)

Suspension From Class by a Teacher

A teacher may suspend a student from his or her class for the day of the suspension as well as the following day for any of the acts specified in Education Code section 48900. (Ed. Code, § 48910, subd. (a).) As noted, this type of suspension may occur only once every five days. (Ed. Code, § 48925, subd. (d)(3).) The teacher must immediately report the suspension to the principal and send the student to the principal or principal's designee for appropriate action. (A principal's designee is one or more school administrators specifically designated in writing by the principal to assist with disciplinary procedures. In the event the school has no administrator in addition to the principal, a certificated school employee may be specifically designated in writing by the principal as a "principal's designee" to assist with disciplinary procedures. The principal may designate only one such person at a time as his or her primary designee for the school year.) (Ed. Code, § 48911, subd. (j).)

As soon as possible, the teacher must also request a parent-teacher conference to discuss the suspension with the student's parent or guardian. Where feasible, a school counselor or psychologist should attend this meeting. A school administrator must also attend if requested to do so by the teacher or the parent or guardian. The student may not return to the teacher's class during the suspension period without the permission of the teacher and the principal. (Ed. Code, § 48910, subd. (a).)

Students suspended from class will not be allowed to attend another regular class during the period of suspension. However, if a student attends more than one class per day, this stipulation only applies to other regular classes scheduled at the same time as the class from which he or she was suspended. (Ed. Code, § 48910, subd. (b).)

If the basis for a student's suspension from class is profanity/obscenity or disruption/defiance, the teacher may request that the student's parent or guardian spend part of the school day in his or her child's classroom. (Ed. Code, § 48900.1.) School district governing boards are directed to adopt policy and procedures to implement this law. The law states that the parent must attend class; however, there is no sanction for failure to do so.

Suspension From School by a Principal, Principal's Designee or Superintendent

A teacher may also send a student to the principal or principal's designee for consideration of a school suspension for any of the acts specified in Education Code section 48900. (Ed. Code, § 48910, subd. (c).)

A principal, principal's designee or superintendent may suspend a student for an offense for up to five consecutive school days. (Ed. Code, § 48911, subd. (a).) Before a suspension is imposed, an informal conference must be held with the principal, principal's designee or superintendent and, whenever possible, the referring teacher or supervisor. At the conference, the student must be informed of the charges against him or her. If the student denies the charges, the incriminating circumstances must be explained, and the student given an opportunity to present his or her version. (Ed. Code, § 48911, subd. (b).)

Emergency situations. A student may be suspended without being given an opportunity for a conference only if the principal, principal's designee or superintendent determines there is an emergency situation that "constitutes a clear and present danger to the life, safety or health of pupils or school personnel." (Ed. Code, § 48911, subd. (c).) If a suspension occurs without a conference, the student and his or her parent or guardian must be notified that the student is entitled to have such a meeting and has the right to return to school for that purpose. The conference must be held within two school days unless the student waives this right or is physically unable to attend, in which case it must be held as soon as possible. (*Goss v. Lopez* (1975) 419 U.S. 565, 581-583; Ed. Code, § 48911, subd. (c).)

Alternatives to Off-Campus Suspensions

In 1994, the Legislature encouraged schools to examine alternatives to off-campus suspensions that would resolve the problem of student misconduct without sending students off campus. If the number of students suspended in the previous school year exceeds more than 30 percent of enrollment, schools should consider implementing at least one of the following: 1) an in-house supervised suspension program; or 2) an alternative to the school's off-campus suspension program involving a progressive discipline approach on campus during the school day. Progressive discipline would use any of the following activities: conferences between school staff, parents and pupils; referral to the school counselor, psychologist, child welfare attendance personnel or other school support service staff; detention; or study, guidance, resource panel or other assessment-related teams. (Ed. Code, § 48911.2.)

Assignment to supervised suspension classroom. A student who is suspended from school for any of the reasons specified in Education Code sections 48900 and 48900.2 may be assigned by the principal or principal's designee to a supervised suspension classroom for the entire suspension period if the student poses no imminent danger or threat to the campus, students or staff or if no action for expulsion has been initiated. This does not include suspensions based on hate violence or harassment. (Ed. Code, §§ 48900.3, 48900.4.) Students assigned to a supervised suspension classroom must be kept apart from their classmates for the suspension period in a separate classroom or building for students under suspension. (Ed. Code, § 48911.1, subds. (a) & (b).)

When a student is assigned to a supervised suspension classroom, a school employee must notify the student's parent or guardian in person or by telephone. If this classroom assignment is for more than one class period, written notification must be provided to the parent or guardian. (Ed. Code, § 48911.1, subd. (d).)

School districts may continue to claim apportionments for each student attending a supervised suspension classroom provided: 1) the classroom is staffed according to the law; 2) each student has access to counseling; 3) completion of schoolwork and tests missed by the student during his or her suspension is promoted; and 4) each student contacts his or her teacher or teachers for assignments to be completed while the student attends the supervised suspension classroom. Teachers must provide all assignments and tests that a student will miss during the suspension. If no classroom work is assigned, the suspension classroom supervisor must assign schoolwork. (Ed. Code, § 48911.1, subd. (c).)

Additional alternatives. A school district may also transfer a suspended student to an opportunity school or class or a continuation education school or class. (Ed. Code, § 48911.1, subd. (e).)

Expulsion

Expulsion is the most serious disciplinary action that a school district may impose on a student. It can only occur through action by the school district governing board. Due process procedures for student expulsion are prescribed in the Education Code. Expulsion is defined as the "removal of a pupil from (1) the immediate supervision and control, or (2) the general supervision of school personnel. . . . " (Ed. Code, § 48925, subd. (b).)

When an explusion takes place, the student is removed from the specific campus from which the offense occurred. The student is then placed into a community school or alternative placement. If the expulsion order is suspended, the student is still placed at another school - not back in the same school where the offense took place.

A student is entitled to a hearing within 30 school days after the principal or superintendent determines that the student has committed any of the specified acts for expulsion, unless he or she requests, in writing, that the hearing be postponed. The student must receive written notice of the hearing at least ten calendar days before the hearing date.[17] (Ed. Code, § 48918, subd. (a).) Expulsion hearings may be conducted by the governing board or before a hearing officer or administrative panel. However, the final decision to expel a student may only be made by the governing board in public session. (Ed. Code, § 48918, subd. (j).)

Mandatory Recommendation for Expulsion

The principal or superintendent must recommend the expulsion if the student has been involved in any of the following at school or at an off-campus school activity:

- Causing serious injury to another person, except in self-defense.
- Possession of a knife, explosive or other dangerous object of no reasonable use to the student.
- Unlawful possession of any controlled substance specified in Health and Safety Code, Division 10, Chapter 2.
- Extortion or robbery.
- Assault or battery, as defined by Penal Code 240 and 242, upon any school employee.

If a student expulsion is found to be inappropriate due to particular circumstances, the principal or superintendent must make a written incident report supporting this recommendation to the governing board. (Ed. Code, § 48915, subd. (a).)

Possession of Firearms: Mandatory Expulsion or Alternative Study Program

When a principal or school superintendent and governing board confirm that a student was knowingly in possession of a firearm or brandishing a knife, and the school district has verified this fact, the board must either expel the student or refer him or her to an

---

[17] See Education Code section 48918 for further specificity on right of postponement, what the notice should contain, how the hearing should be conducted, etc.

alternative study program for students with discipline problems. Students who are expelled for the mandatory offenses under subdivision (c) of Education Code section 48915 will be expelled for up to one full year from the date of expulsion. The program must be provided at a location other than the school site attended by the student at the time the expulsion was recommended. (Ed. Code, § 48915, subds. (b) & (c).) (A student who is authorized to have a firearm by a teacher, school administrator or principal is exempted from the requirements of this section.) The Legislature intended that the governing board request the county board of education to enroll the student in a county community school or a community day school whenever such opportunities exist. (Ed. Code, § 48915.2.)

Discretionary Expulsions Under Specified Circumstances

Upon a recommendation from the principal, school superintendent, hearing officer or administrative panel, the governing board may order a student expelled if he or she has committed one of the acts listed below and either of the following is true: 1) other means of correction are not feasible or have repeatedly failed to produce proper conduct; or 2) due to the nature of the violation, the student's presence continues to endanger his or her physical safety or that of others. Grounds for expulsion include:
- Damaging or stealing school or private property.
- Smoking or using profanity, obscenity or paraphernalia.
- Disrupting school or classroom activities or exhibiting defiance.
- Knowingly receiving stolen school or private property.
- Committing acts of sexual harassment or hate violence. (Ed. Code, §§ 48915, subd. (d); 48900, subds. (f) - (o); 48900.2; 48900.3; 48900.4.)

Suspension of Expulsion
Other Terms and Conditions of Expulsion

Suspension of enforcement. Upon voting to expel a student, the governing board may suspend the enforcement of the expulsion order for up to one calendar year, during which time the student will be classified as being on probation. Also, as a condition of suspending the enforcement, the board may assign the student to an appropriate school, class or program for his or her rehabilitation. Upon satisfactory completion of the rehabilitation assignment, the governing board must reinstate the student in a district school. The board may also order that any or all records of the expulsion proceedings be erased. Suspension of enforcement criteria must be applied equally to all students. (Ed. Code, § 48917, subds. (a) & (b).)

A suspension of an expulsion order may be revoked by the governing board if the student has committed any of the acts listed in Education Code section 48900 or violated any of the district's rules and regulations governing student conduct. Upon revocation of the suspension of an expulsion order, a student may be expelled under the terms of the original expulsion order. (Ed. Code, § 48917, subd. (d).) A record of the expulsion order and its causes must be placed in the student's mandatory interim file. (Ed. Code, § 48918, subd. (k).)

Rehabilitation. The governing board may recommend a rehabilitation plan for the student, which may include, but is not be limited to, periodic review and assessment when he or she applies for readmission. Recommendations for counseling, employment, community service or other rehabilitative programs may also be included. (Ed. Code, § 48916.) A student who is expelled from school for reasons relating to controlled substances or alcohol may be required by the board to enroll in a county-supported drug rehabilitation program before returning to school. However, no student is required to enroll in such a program without the consent of a parent or guardian. (Ed. Code, § 48916.5.)

Date for readmission. If the governing board orders expulsion of a student, it must set a date no later than the last day of the semester following the semester in which the expulsion occurred, and when the student must be reviewed for readmission. A description of the readmission procedure must be made available to the student and his or her parent or guardian at the time the expulsion is ordered. (Ed. Code, § 48916.)

Written Notice of Expulsion and Student Right to Appeal

The superintendent or superintendent's designee must send written notice of any board decision to expel or suspend the enforcement of an expulsion order to the student or his or her parent or guardian. This communication must include information about the student's right to appeal the expulsion to the county board of education. It must also note the obligation of the student, parent or guardian to inform any new school district in which the student enrolls of the expulsion. (Ed. Code, § 48918, subds. (i) & (j).)

Any appeal of a governing board action must be filed with the county board of education within 30 days of the board's original vote. (Ed. Code, § 48917.) A decision of the governing board to suspend an expulsion order will not affect the time period and requirements for filing an appeal of the expulsion order with the county board of education, as required under Education Code section 48919.

The county board of education must hold a hearing within 20 school days after a formal appeal is filed. The board must render a decision within three school days of the hearing, unless the student requests a postponement. (Ed. Code, § 48919.)

Readmission Process

Each school district governing board must establish rules and regulations for filing and processing readmission requests. At the time of expulsion, the governing board must set a date when the student must be reviewed for readmission to the school the student last attended, or to another school maintained by the district. However, after completion of the readmission process, the governing board must readmit the student unless it finds that the student has not met the conditions of his or her rehabilitation plan or poses continuing danger to school safety. (Ed. Code, § 48916, subd. (c).) Readmission options for any expelled student will depend on the severity of the grounds for expulsion and when readmission is sought.

Readmission After Term of Expulsion

During the expulsion period, a student who is expelled for any of the offenses previously outlined under the heading, "Mandatory Recommendation for Expulsion," in this chapter will only be permitted to enroll in a county community school, juvenile court school or community day school. (Ed. Code §§ 48915, subd. (a); 48915.2, subd. (a); 48916.1.)

Enrollment in same school district. By the last day of the semester following the semester in which the expulsion occurred, a student who has been expelled may apply for readmission to another district school. But, as noted, after completion of the readmission process, the governing board is not required to readmit the student. (Ed. Code, § 48916.)

Enrollment in another school district. If a school district governing board receives a request from a student who has been expelled from another district for an act other than those listed under Education Code section 48915, subdivision (a), it must hold a hearing to determine whether the individual poses a danger either to the students or employees of the new school district. (Ed. Code, §§ 48915, subd. (a); 48915.1, subd. (a).)

The district receiving the request has five working days from the date it is received to respond. The hearing and notice must follow the rules and regulations governing procedures for student expulsions as described in Education Code section 48918. The new school district may request information from the previous district concerning a recommendation for expulsion or the expulsion of a student applying for enrollment. (Ed. Code, § 48915.1, subd. (a).)

After a hearing has been held, a decision may be made that the individual expelled from the other school district does not pose a danger to either students or school district employees. In this case, the governing board must permit the student to enroll in one of its district schools after the term of the expulsion, subject to one of the following conditions: 1) legal residence has been established in the school district; or 2) enrollment in the school has been arranged in compliance with an interdistrict agreement. (Ed. Code, § 48915.2, subd. (b).)

Readmission During Term of Expulsion

In deciding whether or not to enroll a student who has been expelled from another district, a governing board may: 1) deny enrollment; 2) permit enrollment; or 3) conditionally permit enrollment in a regular school program or another educational program. (Ed. Code, § 48915.1, subd. (d).)

A school district governing board may deny enrollment to an individual expelled from another school district for any act listed in Education Code section 48915, subdivision (a) for the remainder of the expulsion period if, after holding a hearing, it determines that the "individual poses a potential danger to either the pupils or employees of the school district." (Ed. Code, § 48915.1, subd. (c).) Or, the decision may be made that the student does not pose a danger to other students or employees. In this case, the governing board must permit the student to enroll in one of its district schools during the term of the expulsion, subject to one of the following conditions: 1) legal residence has been established in the school district; or 2) enrollment in the school has been arranged in compliance with an agreement between the affected school districts. (Ed. Code, § 48915.1, subd. (e).)

After enrollment in the new district is completed, a student who has been expelled from another school district must inform the new district of his or her previous status. If this information is not provided, and it is later determined that the student was expelled from the previous school, his or her failure to furnish the information must be recorded and discussed at a hearing, as previously outlined under the subheading, "Enrollment in Another School District," in this chapter. (Ed. Code, § 48915.1, subd. (b).)

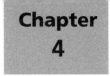
The Limits of Discipline

This chapter focuses on the relationship between constitutional rights and the enforcement of discipline at school.

Teachers and administrators must balance their disciplinary policies and procedures against the constitutional rights of students, school employees and other individuals in the community who interact with the schools. At the same time, it is imperative that those who are delegated the important duty of school administrator make it clear that personal responsibility for respectful and orderly behavior will be the school's culture.

The First Amendment to the U.S. Constitution provides that "Congress shall make no law respecting an establishment of religion, or prohibiting the free exercise thereof; or abridging the freedom of speech, or of the press; or the right of the people peaceably to assemble, and to petition the Government for a redress of grievances." Demonstrations, picketing, political activity and other expressions of personal opinions presented through school activities or publications may involve First Amendment protection.

Nevertheless, school administrators have several legal tools at their disposal to ensure campus and student safety. One of these tools is case law. This area of the law is in a constant state of "change," therefore, it is incumbent on school officials to familiarize themselves with the rudimentary working knowledge in this area.

In *Tinker v. Des Moines Independent Community School District*, the U.S. Supreme Court made this point:

> "[S]tudents or teachers do not shed their constitutional rights to freedom of speech or expression at the schoolhouse gate. . . . [A student] may express his [or her]

opinions, even on controversial subjects, if he [or she] does so without materially and substantially interfering with the requirements of others. . . . But conduct by . . . [a] student in class or out of it, which for any reason . . . whether it stems from time, place, or type of behavior which . . . materially disrupts class work or involves substantial disorder, or invasion of the rights of others is . . . not immunized by the constitutional guarantee of free speech." (*Tinker v. Des Moines Independent Community School District* (1969) 393 U.S. 503, 506.)

Constitutional Rights and California Law

The same restrictions on regulations concerning speech, religion and association that limit the federal government under the First Amendment apply to the states under the Fourteenth Amendment.[18] The right of students to free expression is thus constitutional and statutory. According to the California Constitution, "Every person may freely speak, write and publish his or her sentiments on all subjects, being responsible for the abuse of this right. A law may not restrain or abridge liberty of speech or press." (Cal. Const., art. I, § 2, subd. (a).)

Laws Governing Free Speech on School Grounds

Education Code section 48907 further provides for the following:

"Students of the public schools shall have the right to exercise freedom of speech and of the press including, but not limited to, the use of bulletin boards, the distribution of printed materials or petitions, the wearing of buttons, badges, and other insignia, and the right of expression in official publications, whether or not such publications or other means of expression are supported financially by the school or by use of school facilities, except that expression

---

[18] *West Virginia State Board of Education v. Barnette* (1943) 319 U.S. 624; *Everson v. Board of Education* (1947) 330 U.S. 1; *Edwards v. South Carolina* (1963) 372 U.S. 229.

shall be prohibited which is obscene, libelous, or slanderous. Also prohibited shall be material which so incites students as to create a clear and present danger of the commission of unlawful acts on school premises or the violation of lawful school regulations, or the substantial disruption of the orderly operation of the school.

Each governing board of a school district and each county board of education shall adopt rules and regulations as a written publications code, which shall include reasonable provisions for the time, place, and manner of conducting such activities within its respective jurisdiction."

In 1992, lawmakers added section 48950 to the Education Code, thereby protecting the rights of public high school students to engage in constitutionally protected speech or other communications. Public and private high schools are prohibited from making and enforcing disciplinary rules against students solely based on speech or other communications if the First Amendment of the Constitution or Article 1, section 2 of the California Constitution would protect the conduct from governmental restriction off campus. If a high school unfairly tries to control freedom of speech, a student may pursue a civil action to "obtain appropriate injunctive and declaratory relief as determined by the court (prohibit the school from restricting freedom of speech)." However, "free speech rights are subject to reasonable time, place, and manner regulations." (Ed. Code, § 48950, subds. (a), (b) & (f).)

This does not prohibit schools from disciplining students for harassment, threats or intimidation, unless these actions are constitutionally protected; nor does it replace or otherwise limit or modify the provisions of Education Code section 48907. Although applicable to private schools, the law does not require private schools controlled by religious organizations to permit speech that is in opposition to their fundamental religious beliefs. (Ed. Code, § 48950, subds. (c), (d) & (e).)

Right of Students to Address School Personnel

Students, parents, teachers and administrators should encourage respectful dialogue about problems between students and school personnel. Teachers and other school officials should make a concerted effort to allow students the freedom and opportunity to speak freely with them on any subject or issue. By allowing students this flexibility, some portions of criticisms spoken may be miscon-strued or taken negatively by school personnel. However, this type of criticism, providing it is constructive, should be acceptable from students and falls under the concept of fair comment. Teachers and administrators should not retaliate and stifle fair comment, but consider the dialogue and objectives on their own merits.

In addition, teachers and administrators must preserve the dignity of confidential information and maintain the integrity of any state-ments made to them in confidence by students. Careless repetition by school personnel of such conversations can make a solvable incident or situation unsolvable and potentially dangerous to every-one involved, especially if the discussion involves illegal activity or plans for criminal behavior.

Protected Activities

Literature Distribution

The Education Code grants students the right to distribute printed materials or petitions and make use of bulletin boards. (Ed. Code, § 48907.) California courts have also recognized this as a funda-mental right. *In Mandel v. Municipal Court*, the Court of Appeal stated, "The protection of the First and Fourteenth Amendments extends to the distribution of information and opinion concerning religious, political and economic matters, and other subjects of public concern through handbills, leaflets, and pamphlets." (*Mandel v. Municipal Court* (1969) 276 Cal.App.2d 649, 665.)

The Mandel case also demonstrated that adults have the right to come onto school campuses for the purpose of distributing such literature. In this instance, an adult passed out anti-draft pamphlets that urged students to attend a meeting and outlined a proposal for a one-day student strike. (*Id.* at p. 649.) In another case, People v. Hirst, the appellate court ruled that an adult had the right to stay on campus and talk to students even after his supply of literature ran out. (*People v. Hirst* (1973) 31 Cal.App.3d 75.) It was noted in Hirst, however, that school authorities retain the right to: 1) prevent disruption and disorder; and 2) forbid or control — in a nondiscriminatory manner — hand billing on school grounds by individuals who are not students, teachers or administrators. (*Burch v. Barker* (9th Cir. 1988) 861 F.2nd. 1149.)

The State has power to preserve the property under its control for its intended use. The United States Constitution does not prevent a State from restricting that use to its own lawful nondiscriminatory purpose.

Regulation may extend to nonstudent activity on public or private property adjacent to school grounds if the activity is carried on in such manner as to disturb or tend to disturb the peace or good order of the school session even though the activity otherwise comes within the protection of the First Amendment (*Grayned v. City of Rockford* (1972) 408 U.S. 104).

In Grayned the court made these observations: "[We] think it clear that the public sidewalk adjacent to school grounds may not be declared off-limits for expressive activity by members of the public. But in each case, expressive activity may be prohibited if it 'materially disrupts classwork or involves substantial disorder or invasion of the rights of others ...'" Tinker v. Des Moines School District, 393 U.S. at 513.

School Publications
The Education Code protects the rights of students to exercise freedom of the press, as long as publications are not obscene, libelous or slanderous, or do not present a clear and present danger of inciting students to commit unlawful acts on school premises. (Ed. Code, § 48907.)

Student editors of official school publications such as newspapers, yearbooks or other material distributed to the student body are responsible for assigning and editing the news, feature and opinion content, subject to the limitations of Education Code section 48907. It is the responsibility of the journalism adviser of a school publication to supervise its production by the student staff, maintain professional standards of English and journalism and uphold the provisions of the Education Code.

Finally, the code provides that "[t]here shall be no prior restraint of material prepared for official school publications except insofar as it violates this section." School officials must justify any limitations without "undue delay" before imposing restrictions on student expression. (Ed. Code, § 48907.)

In 1988, the U.S. Supreme Court held that educators acted reasonably in deleting two pages of student articles about pregnancy and divorce from a publicly-funded high school newspaper. Educators do not violate the First Amendment by exercising editorial control over the style and content of student speech in school-sponsored expressive activities, provided that they can reasonably relate their actions to legitimate educational concerns. Here, the school newspaper was not a public forum, but part of the educational curriculum. A school need not tolerate student speech that is inconsistent with its basic educational mission, although the government cannot censor speech outside the school. (*Hazelwood School District v. Kuhlmeier* (1988) 484 U.S. 260, 98 L.Ed.2d 592, 108 S.Ct. 562.)

Demonstrations

The U.S. Supreme Court has recognized the right of students to publicize their grievances in a peaceful, nondisruptive manner on school campuses. (*Grayned v. City of Rockford* (1972) 408 U.S. 104) Individuals who are not students also have the right to picket on public sidewalks adjacent to school grounds. (*Id.* at p. 118.) A California case emphasized this point by declaring that the sidewalks adjacent to schools and elsewhere "are dedicated in part for meeting people and exchanging ideas. Thus, neither the picketer nor pedestrian has a superior right of way. These interests must be weighed and balanced." (*People v. Horton* (1970) 9 Cal.App.3d Supp. 1, 9.)

While limitations on the right to picket and other free-speech rights will be discussed later, it should be noted here that the right to picket does not extend to interfering with pedestrian traffic or motorist right of way.[19]

Refusing to Salute the Flag

The U.S. Supreme Court has held that schools may not force students to salute the American flag. Since that decision, several school districts have tried to require children who declined to salute the flag to at least stand for the salute. The federal courts have been unanimous in holding that such requirements are unconstitutional. (*West Virginia State Board of Education v. Barnette* (1943) 319 U.S. 624.)

For example, when a school board announced that students who chose not to salute the flag should stand quietly or leave the room during the salute, one student refused to stand. The circuit court of appeals held that the child's refusal was a form of expression; he was exercising a right similar to pure speech. (*Goetz v. Ansell* (2d Cir. 1973) 477 F.2d 636; *Sheldon v. Fannin* (D. Ariz. 1963) 221 F.Supp. 766; *Fran v. Baron* (E.D. N.Y. 1969) 307 F.Supp. 27.)

Furthermore, a student's right to free expression may not be limited merely because that expression may lead other students to exercise their rights. In one case, school authorities complained that a student's refusal to stand and salute the flag had persuaded others to take the same action. The U.S. District Court dismissed this argument and observed that "'[t]he First Amendment protects successful dissent as well as ineffective protests.'" (*Hanover v. Northrup* (D. Conn. 1970) 325 F.Supp. 170, 173, quoting *Frain v. Baron* (E.D. N.Y. 1969) 307 F.Supp. 27.)

---

[19] *People v. Horton* (1970) 9 Cal.App.3d, Supp. 1, 10; Penal Code section 647c (obstruction of free movement on street, sidewalk or public place); Penal Code section 370 (public nuisance); Vehicle Code section 21954 (pedestrians outside sidewalks).

In another example, a teacher refused to lead or recite the Pledge of Allegiance, choosing instead to remain seated with her head bowed. (36 U.S.C., § 172.) School officials charged her with insubordination. The federal court held that she had a constitutional right to remain seated and refuse to lead the pledge. (*Hanover v. Northrup, supra*, 325 F.Supp. at p. 170.)

Objecting to Dissection or Other Harmful Use of Animals

California law allows any student with a moral objection to dissecting or otherwise harming or destroying animals to choose not to participate in this kind of education project. Teachers who use live or dead animals or animal parts in their courses must notify students of their rights under this law. Agricultural classes and activities that provide instruction on the care, management and evaluation of domestic animals are exempt from these provisions. (Ed. Code, § 32255.6.) A note from a parent or guardian must confirm the student's objection.

The teacher may give an alternate project to the student, but may not penalize him or her with a more difficult assignment. The student must pass the same tests required of other students, unless the tests require the harmful or destructive use of animals. In that case, the teacher may give the student an alternative test. (Ed. Code, §§ 32255 *et seq.*)

The Limits of Free Expression

Even if an activity amounts to "speech" or "expression," a school may still prohibit or regulate the activity if: 1) it creates a clear and present danger of substantial disruption; 2) it contains prohibited content; or 3) the school is not completely prohibiting the activity, but merely regulating the "time, place or manner in which it is conducted." (Ed. Code, § 48907.)

California law allows suspension or expulsion of students for various offenses, including threats, extortion, obscenity, profanity or disruption of school activities. (Ed. Code, § 48900.) Students in grades 4-12 may be disciplined for sexual harassment. As noted in Chapter 5, sexual harassment occurs when conduct is such that it negatively impacts an individual's work, academic performance or educational environment. (Ed. Code, § 48900.2.) Harassment, threats or intimidation against a student or group of students can also be the basis for student discipline in grades 4-12. Such harassment must be "sufficiently severe or pervasive to have the actual and reasonably expected effect of materially disrupting classwork, creating substantial disorder, and invading the rights of that pupil or group of pupils by creating an intimidating or hostile educational environment." (Ed. Code, § 48900.4.)

Activities Creating a Clear and Present Danger

Schools may prohibit an activity if it "so incites students as to create a clear and present danger of the commission of unlawful acts on school premises, or the violation of lawful school regulations, or the substantial disruption of the orderly operation of the school." (Ed. Code, § 48907.) The danger, however, must rise "far above public inconvenience, annoyance or unrest." (*Mandel v. Municipal Court, supra,* 276 Cal.App.2d. at p. 669.)

This standard requires administrators to possess facts, rather than rely on speculations or opinions, in establishing that substantial danger is "clear and present." The U.S. Supreme Court emphasized this requirement in strong language:

> "[I]n our system, undifferentiated fear or apprehension of disturbance is not enough to overcome the right to freedom of expression. Any departure from absolute regimentation may cause trouble. Any variation from the majority's opinion may inspire fear. Any words spoken in class, in the lunchroom, or on the campus, that deviates from the views of another person may start an argument or cause a disturbance. But our Constitution says we must take this risk; and our history says that it is this sort of

hazardous freedom — this kind of openness — that is the basis of our national strength and of the independence and vigor of Americans who grow up and live in this relatively permissive, often disputatious, society." (*Tinker v. Des Moines School District, supra*, 393 U.S. at pp. 503, 508.)

For instance, students are ordinarily entitled to wear symbols of dissent, but these symbols may be banned if they cause "material and substantial interference with the requirements of appropriate discipline in the operation of the school." (*Id.* at p. 506.) In other cases, however, courts have upheld bans on such symbols. (*Guzick v. Drebis* (6th Cir. 1970) 431 F.2d 594; *Hill v. Lewis* (E.D. N.C. 1971) 323 F.Supp. 55; *Hernandez v. School District No. 1* (D. Col. 1970) 315 F.Supp. 289.)

Likewise, while peaceful demonstrations are lawful, "schools could hardly tolerate boisterous demonstrators who drown out classroom conversation, make studying impossible, block entrances, or incite children to leave the schoolhouse." (*Grayned v. City of Rockford, supra,* 408 U.S. at p. 119.) In addition, literature that can be shown to have substantially disrupted or interfered with school procedures may be banned, and its disseminators punished. In the absence of such evidence, schools may take no disciplinary action. (*Scoville v. Board of Education* (7th Cir. 1970) 425 F.2d 10; see also *Katz v. McAvlavlag* (2nd Cir. 1971) 438 F.2d 1058.)

To avoid a "chilling effect" on free speech, a school administrator should not threaten to prosecute for "disturbing or breaking up any assembly or meeting" unless it seems clear to the teacher or administrator that the disruption goes beyond the constitutionally protected right of free speech. If the disruptive act is sufficiently extreme, it may constitute "disturbing the peace." (*Bethel School District No. 43 v. Fraser* (1986) 478 U.S. 675, 106 S.Ct. 3159, 92 L.Ed.2d 549; Pen. Code, § 403.)

Unprotected Speech

The U.S. Constitution does not protect obscene, libelous or slanderous speech. (*Grayned v. City of Rockford, supra,* 408 U.S. at p. 115.) With regard to student rights, the Education Code prohibits obscene, libelous or slanderous expression. (Ed. Code, § 48907.)

In *Bethel School District No. 43 v. Fraser,* a student was disciplined for giving a nominating speech for a fellow student, the "entirety" of which was replete with "elaborate, graphic, and explicit sexual metaphor." Noting that the speech was vulgar, embarrassing to the 14-year-old students in the audience and insulting to the females in attendance, the U.S. Supreme Court upheld the right of school officials to discipline the speaker. The court stated that the First Amendment did not forbid school officials from punishing vulgar and lewd speech that "undermines the school's basic educational mission." (*Bethel School District No. 43 v. Fraser, supra,* 478 U.S. at p. 675.)

In *Lopez v. Tulare Joint Union High School District Board of Trustees,* the California Court of Appeal, Fifth Appellate District held that school authorities could delete profanity from a student-produced film because it violated the "professional standards of English and journalism provision of [Education Code] section 48907." In this case, students wrote and produced a film in connection with a Film Arts class. The dialogue included profane expressions and references to sexual activity to make the film characters more realistic and convincing. After script review, the principal and district superintendent found the language "highly offensive and educationally unsuitable" and directed the class instructor to have the students remove the profanity and sexual references. The instructor and the students appealed the directive to the school board, which held that "sound educational policy" as well as district regulation required that the profanity in the film be deleted. (*Lopez v. Tulare Joint Union High School Dist.* (1995) 34 Cal.App.4th 1302, 40 Cal.Rptr.2d 762.)

School Dress Codes

In 1994, the Legislature decided that "[t]he adoption of a school-wide uniform policy is a reasonable way to provide some protection for students. A required uniform may protect students from being associated with any particular gang. Moreover, by requiring school-wide uniforms teachers and administrators may not need to occupy as much of their time learning the subtleties of gang regalia. . . . " (Ed. Code, § 35183, subd. (a)(5).)

School district governing boards may adopt (or rescind) a reasonable dress code policy requiring students to wear a uniform at school. The principal, staff and parents from each individual school must initiate the plan within the district. The board must determine that the policy is "necessary for the health and safety of the school environment." (Ed. Code, § 35183, subd. (b).) Individual schools may include a reasonable dress code policy as part of their school safety plan. (Ed. Code, § 35294.1.)

The policy must include a provision that no student will be penalized academically, discriminated against or denied attendance to school if his or her parents choose not to have the student comply with the school uniform policy. In addition, adoption of a schoolwide uniform policy must not keep students who participate in nationally recognized youth organizations from wearing special uniforms on the days their group has a scheduled meeting. (Ed. Code, § 35183, subds. (f) & (g).)

If schoolwide uniforms are required, the principal, staff and parents at each school will select the specific uniform. Before implementing a dress code policy requiring uniforms, at least six months' notice must be given to parents, and resources to assist economically disadvantaged students must be made available. (Ed. Code, § 35183, subds. (c), (d) & (e).)

Dress codes must clearly describe the type of apparel that is prohibited. Schools may prohibit students from wearing "gang-related apparel" as part of their school safety plan. (Ed. Code, § 35294.1.)

Gang-related apparel is limited to apparel that, if worn or displayed on a school campus would be determined to threaten the health and safety of the school environment. (Ed. Code, § 35183 subd. (a)(2).)

A Southern California school board adopted a dress code policy that restricted students from wearing clothing bearing writing, pictures or insignia which identified any professional sports team or college on school district campuses or at school functions. The policy was challenged by students in the district's elementary, middle and high schools. The U.S. Court of Appeal heard testimony on the alleged "gang situation" that prompted adoption of the policy. Based on this evidence, the court struck down the policy for elementary and middle school children, but upheld its legality for high school students.[20]

Drug Testing

School districts may lawfully require, as a condition of student participation in non-credit, after-school athletic programs, that a student submit to unannounced urine tests for the presence of drugs, if the district has reasonably determined: 1) that drug abuse by student athletes is occurring and does constitute a serious hazard to their safety while they are participating in athletic programs; 2) that the method of testing employed is designed to detect the types of drugs which constitute the hazard; and 3) that no effective, but less onerous (troublesome) method of preventing the drug abuse is available. If the student is a minor, his or her parents or guardian must give written consent for the student to take the tests. (62 Ops.Cal.Atty.Gen. 344 (1979).)

In a 1995 case decision, the U.S. Supreme Court determined that school district policies authorizing urinalysis drug testing of students who participated in the district's athletics programs did not violate the federal Constitution's Fourth Amendment. Urine samples are

---

[20] *Jeglin v. San Jacinto Unified School District* (1993) 827 F.Supp. 1459. See also Paul D. Murphy, *Restricting Gang Clothing in Public Schools: Does a Dress Code Violate a Student's Right of Free Expression?* Southern California Law Review, 64 (1991) 1321, 1360-62.

obtained in privacy; the information disclosed is only for drugs, not regarding epileptic, pregnant or diabetic conditions; the drugs for which the samples are screened are standard; test results are disclosed only to a limited class of school personnel who have a need to know; the results are not turned over to law enforcement or used for any internal disciplinary function; and, students must identify in advance any prescription medications to avoid sanctions for a false positive test. (*Vernonia School District. 47J v. Acton* (1995) 515 U.S. 646.)

Extreme Hair Styles

In *Myers v. Arcata, etc., School District,* a regulation forbidding "extreme . . . hair style" was struck down. The Court of Appeal held that this standard was so vague that students could not be sure whether they were in violation. (*Myers v. Arcata, etc., School District* (1969) 269 Cal.App.2d 549.) Being specific, of course, puts a special burden on school officials and may lead to some frustration as juvenile styles change. As one judge lamented, "The long hair case of today may be a shaven head case tomorrow, or a brilliantly dyed hair case of another time. The possible extremes of dress and attire are nearly unlimited." (*Crews v. Cloncs* (S.D. Ind. 1969) 303 F.Supp. 1370, 1374.)

In *Montalvo v. Madera Unified School District Board of Education*, a student challenged a school board regulation specifying the maximum length of hair. The Court of Appeal noted those issues of grooming, including hair style, are not related to "free speech." Grooming codes will be upheld if the schools can show "some reasonable relationship between the legitimate concerns of the school administration relating to the education process" and the "rules controlling the length and style of male hair." The court held that the rule was reasonable in this case. (*Montalvo v. Madera Unified School District Board of Education* (1971) 21 Cal.App.3d 323.)[21]

---

[21] See also *Jeffers v. Yuba City Unified School District* (E.D.Cal. 1970) 319 F.Supp. 368; *Olff v. East Side Union High School District* (N.D. Cal. 1969) 305 F.Supp. 557.

Regulation of Time, Place and Manner

As previously noted, Education Code section 48907 requires each governing board and county superintendent to adopt rules and regulations concerning the exercise of free expression "which shall include reasonable provisions for the time, place and manner of conducting such activities." The rationale behind this statute has long been recognized by the courts. As the U.S. Supreme Court stated:

> "For example, two parades cannot march on the same street simultaneously, and government may allow only one. A demonstration or parade on a large street during rush hour might put an intolerable burden on the essential flow of traffic, and for that reason could be prohibited. If overamplified loudspeakers assault the citizenry, government may turn them down. Subject to such reasonable regulation, however, peaceful demonstrations in public places are protected by the First Amendment. Of course, where demonstrations turn violent, they lose their protected quality as expression under the First Amendment.
>
> The nature of a place, the pattern of its normal activities, dictate the kinds of regulations of time, place and manner that are reasonable. Although a silent vigil may not unduly interfere with a public library, making a speech in the reading room almost certainly would. That same speech should be perfectly appropriate in a park. The crucial question is whether the manner of expression is basically incompatible with the normal activity of a particular place at a particular time." (*Grayned v. City of Rockford, supra,* 408 U.S. at pp. 115-116.)

Regulations of time, place or manner must meet three tests. First, they must be narrowly drawn to channel speech — rather than to eliminate it — in such a manner that they do not interfere with other important interests. As the U.S. Supreme Court stated, "[f]ree expression 'must not, in the guise of regulation, be abridged or denied.'" (*Grayned v. City of Rockford, supra,* 408 U.S. at p. 117.) This is what the California Legislature meant when it specified that such provisions must be "reasonable." (Ed. Code, § 48907.)

Second, the regulations must use objective standards to clearly define prohibited areas; vague laws offend several important values. Because it is assumed that people are free to choose between lawful and unlawful conduct, society insists that laws give people of ordinary intelligence a reasonable opportunity to know what is prohibited, so that they may act accordingly. Vague laws may trap the innocent by not providing fair warning. And, if arbitrary and discriminatory enforcement is to be prevented, laws must provide explicit standards for those who apply them.

Third, the regulations must not discriminate. (*Sullivan v. Houston Ind. School District* (S.D. Tex. 1969) 307 F.Supp. 1328, 1340.) For instance, school authorities cannot allow a group opposed to American foreign policy to use the public address system for a rally, but the next day prohibit access to the equipment to an organization that supports the policy.

Although Education Code section 48907 gives students the right to use bulletin boards, governing boards may adopt regulations that prohibit posting handbills with gummed backs on the bulletin boards, or posting materials in locations other than bulletin boards, because these actions violate time, place and manner regulations.

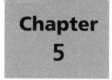

Crime on Campus

While educators observe a wide variety of student behavior on a daily basis, they may sometimes be unsure whether or not the behavior is criminal. If an act constitutes a criminal violation in the community, it is also a criminal violation when it occurs on campus. Criminal behavior must be dealt with by teachers, administrators and, where warranted, by law enforcement authorities. To control and eliminate harmful, disruptive behavior at school, teachers, school safety personnel and administrators must respond to all school crime.

Accordingly, students involved in criminal behavior must receive swift and consistent consequences through school disciplinary measures and, as appropriate, immediate referral to local law enforcement or juvenile officials. Also, school administrators need to make parents and guardians aware of their civil liability for criminal acts committed by students for whom they are responsible.

This chapter is designed to help educators recognize common criminal violations and acquaint school administrators, parents and guardians with state liability laws for injuries resulting from these acts.

Felonies, Misdemeanors and Infractions

Criminal violations are categorized as felonies, misdemeanors or infractions. A felony is a crime punishable by imprisonment in the state prison or death. Every other crime or public offense is a misdemeanor except those offenses classified as infractions. (Pen. Code, § 17, subd. (a).) A misdemeanor may carry a penalty of a fine and/or a county jail sentence of up to one year. An infraction results solely in a fine. Some crimes are punishable as either misdemeanors or felonies, depending on the severity of the offense and/or the offender's criminal record.

In California, the county district attorney's office ultimately decides whether the violator will be charged with a misdemeanor or felony. The classification of a crime as a misdemeanor or a felony is significant. For example, the classification of the violation sets the parameters under which a teacher or other civilian may make a "private person's arrest." (See "Arrests by a Private Citizen" in Chapter 6.)

The most common criminal violations occurring on school campuses are presented here with appropriate code citations. Crime categories include threats and physical violence, weapons violations (e.g., firearms and knives), crimes against personal and school property and drug and alcohol violations.

Crimes involving firearms may have severe consequences for 14 to 17-year-olds, because the perpetrators may be remanded to adult court to face more serious penalties. (Welf. & Inst. Code, § 707.)

Threats and Physical Violence

Traditionally, far more tolerance was shown toward "schoolyard scuffles" and other petty forms of criminal behavior by one person against another. Today, this tolerance level has faded as minor quarrels rapidly escalate into serious violent crimes, including gang-related drive-by or other shootings, violence between boyfriends and girlfriends and hate crimes.   Minors who become victims of crime are sometimes threatened with more violence if they report the incident. Thus, they may be reluctant to report such crimes. Even if a victim tolerates or accepts bullying as a way of life, school staff should not. Whether a criminal action or disciplinary action will be brought about does not necessarily depend on the victim's willingness to press charges. Moreover, a victim or witness cannot refuse to testify in court without facing the possibility of contempt of court charges.

Threats

Intimidation or threatening of witness or victim. Any person who knowingly and maliciously prevents or dissuades any witness or victim from attending or giving testimony at any trial, proceeding or inquiry authorized by law is guilty of a public offense and shall be punished by imprisonment in a county jail or state prison. (Misdemeanor or Felony, Pen. Code, § 136.1, subd. (a)-(b); Felony, Pen. Code, § 136.1, subd. (c).)

Intent to use a deadly weapon to intimidate a witness. Any person, who has upon his person, a deadly weapon with the intent to use such weapon to intimidate a witness is guilty of an offense punishable by imprisonment in the county jail for not than one year, or in the state prison. (Misdemeanor or Felony, Pen. Code, § 136.5.)

Threatening school officers. "Every person who, with intent to cause, attempts to cause, or causes, any officer or employee of any public or private educational institution . . . to do, or refrain from doing, any act in the performance of his duties, by means of a threat, directly communicated to such person, to inflict an unlawful injury upon any person or property, and it reasonably appears to the recipient of the threat that such threat could be carried out, is guilty of a public offense. . . . " (Misdemeanor or Felony, Pen. Code, § 71.)

Example: A class is disrupted by nine students yelling outside the classroom. The teacher asks the students to leave, and one student goes into the classroom and says in an angry and belligerent tone that he will "slap [her] . . . face in." The teacher later testifies that the student could have carried out his threat if he wished to do so. The court holds that it is not necessary to prove that during the incident it reasonably appeared the threat would be carried out; proof it could have been carried out is sufficient. (*In re Zardies B.* (1976) 64 Cal.App.3d 11, 13-14.)

Example: If a teacher hears about Joe's threat to attack his teacher through another student, Joe is not guilty of this crime unless he personally sent the student as a messenger to pass on the threat. (*People v. Zendejas* (1987) 196 Cal.App.3d 367.)

Threatening to commit a crime. "Any person who willfully threatens to commit a crime which will result in death or great bodily injury to another person, with the specific intent that the statement is to be taken as a threat, even if there is no intent of actually carrying it out, which, on its face and under the circumstances in which it is made, is so unequivocal, unconditional, immediate and specific as to convey to the person threatened, a gravity of purpose and an immediate prospect of execution of the threat, and thereby causes that person reasonably to be in sustained fear for his or her own safety or for his or her immediate family's safety. . . . " There is no requirement that the threat be made to influence the performance of a duty, or that it be made directly to the person. (Misdemeanor or Felony, Pen. Code, § 422; Ed. Code, §§ 48900, subd. (o), 48900.7.)

Example: After a series of hostile encounters between Victor and Dave that culminate in a fight at school, Dave tells Wendy that he is going to shoot Victor. Wendy tells Victor about the threat, causing him to fear for his safety. Dave may be arrested and prosecuted for this crime, even though the threat was conveyed to a third party. (*In re David L.* (1991) 234 Cal.App.3d 1655.)

Stalking. "Any person who willfully, maliciously, and repeatedly follows or harasses another person and who makes a credible threat with the intent to place that person in reasonable fear for his or her safety, or the safety of his or her immediate family is guilty of the crime of stalking . . . " "Harasses" means a knowing and willful course of conduct directed at a specific person that seriously alarms, annoys, torments or terrorizes the person, and that serves no legitimate purpose. This course of conduct must be such as would cause a reasonable person to suffer substantial emotional distress, and must actually cause substantial emotional distress to the person. Course of conduct means a pattern of conduct composed of a series of acts over a period of time, however short, evidencing a continuity of purpose. Constitutionally protected activity is not included within the meaning of "course of conduct." Credible threats include threats which are communicated through the use of an electronic communications device, including telephones, cellular phones, computers, video recorders, fax machines and pagers. (Misdemeanor or Felony, Pen. Code, §§ 646.9, subd. (a); 653m.)

Physical Violence

Assault and battery. In addition to the criminal sanctions, Education Code section 48915, subdivision (a) requires the principal to recommend expulsion for a student causing physical injury to another person, except in self-defense.

Assault is "[a]n unlawful attempt, coupled with a present ability, to commit a violent injury on the person of another." (Misdemeanor, Pen. Code, §§ 240, 241.) Other types of assaults include those committed against:

- Anyone on a school campus. (Misdemeanor, Pen. Code, § 241.2.)
- School bus drivers. (Misdemeanor, Pen. Code, § 241.3.)
- Peace officers, firefighters, etc. (Misdemeanor, Pen. Code, § 241, subd. (b).)
- School district peace officers engaged in performance of their duties. (Misdemeanor or Felony, Pen. Code, § 241.4.)
- School employees. (Misdemeanor, Pen. Code, § 241.6.)

Assault crimes also include those committed with a deadly weapon or instrument, firearm, stun gun or taser against a school employee. (Misdemeanor or Felony, Pen. Code, § 245.5.)

Example: Armed with a stick, Michael lunges at Scott, but is stopped by the teacher on duty before he actually touches Scott. Michael is guilty of an assault. There is no requirement that the victim actually suffer bodily harm.

Battery is "any willful and unlawful use of force or violence upon the person of another." (Misdemeanor or Felony, Pen. Code, §§ 242, 243.)

Example: If one child attacks another with fists or a stick, or kicks or shoves him or her, this is considered a criminal battery. Battery only applies to the use of "unlawful" force.

Other types of battery include the following:

- Inflicting injury against a peace officer.
  (Misdemeanor or Felony, Pen. Code, § 243, subd. (c).)
- Inflicting serious bodily injury.
  (Misdemeanor or Felony, Pen. Code, § 243, subd. (d).)
- Using force against a person on school property.
  (Misdemeanor, Pen. Code, § 243.2, subd. (a).)
- Using force against a school bus driver.
  (Misdemeanor or Felony, Pen. Code, § 243.3.)
- Committing sexual battery.
  (Misdemeanor or Felony, Pen. Code, § 243.4.)
- Using force against a school employee.
  (Misdemeanor or Felony, Pen. Code, § 243.6.)[22]
- Using force against a sports official.
  (Misdemeanor, Pen. Code, § 243.8.)

Fighting/disturbing the peace. Punishment is specified for "[a]ny person who unlawfully fights in a public place or challenges another person in a public place to fight . . . [or] maliciously and willfully disturbs another person by loud and unreasonable noise . . . [or] who uses offensive words . . . likely to provoke an immediate violent reaction." (Misdemeanor, Pen. Code, § 415.) When this crime is committed inside a school or on school grounds by someone other than a student or school employee, there is a penalty enhancement. (Misdemeanor, Pen. Code, § 415.5, subd. (a).)

---

[22] School employees may sue the district in federal court for violation of their federal civil rights (42 U.S.C.A. § 1983) if the school fails to protect them from bodily harm. (*Zemsky v. City of New York* (2nd. Cir. 1987) 821 F.2d 148) Staff may not, however, sue for damages under Article I, section 28(c) of the California Constitution. Instead, their only recourse in state court is the worker's compensation law. (*Halliman v. Los Angeles Unified School District* (1984) 163 Cal.App.3d 46.)

Example: If a student challenges another to fight, even if it is not punishable as an assault or battery, the challenge may constitute disturbing the peace. A mutual fight — mutual affray — would also be considered a crime and punishable under this section.

False imprisonment. This means the unlawful violation of the personal liberty of another (Misdemeanor or Felony, Pen. Code, § 236.) and also includes false imprisonment with violence or menace. (Felony, Pen. Code, § 237.) (*People v. Arvanites* (1971) 17 Cal.App.3d 1052.)

Example: If several children surround one child to prevent him or her from leaving, this constitutes false imprisonment. (*People v. Haney* (1977) 75 Cal.App.3d 308, 313.)

Willful disturbance of meeting. It is unlawful to willfully disturb or break up a meeting or assembly without authority. (Misdemeanor, Pen. Code, § 403.)

Material disruption of classwork or extracurricular activities. It is unlawful for any parent, guardian or other person to disrupt classwork or extra-curricular activities, or cause substantial disorder where a school employee is carrying out his or her duties. (Misdemeanor, Ed. Code, §§ 44810, 44811.)

Hazing. It is unlawful for a student or other person attending any educational institution to participate in hazing or "commit any act that causes or is likely to cause bodily danger, physical harm or personal degradation or disgrace resulting in physical or mental harm to any fellow student or person attending the institution." (Misdemeanor, Ed. Code, § 32051.) The language in this section is obviously very broad and covers a number of circumstances. It not only prohibits physical attacks or attempted attacks that would constitute an assault or battery, but also forbids such activities as throwing objects near other students, pulling down another student's pants in public, daring a child to commit a dangerous act and other similar situations.

Firearms, Knives and Other Weapons

The following is a brief summary of crimes involving firearms and other dangerous weapons that may occur on school grounds or at school-sponsored events.

Principals must immediately suspend and recommend expulsion for any student found to be in possession of a firearm at school or at an off-campus school activity. (Ed. Code, § 48915, subd. (c).) The federal Gun-Free Schools Act of 1994 provides that no schools may receive federal funds from Public Law 103-227, the Improving America's Schools Act, unless they have a policy in effect requiring expulsion from school for a period of at least one calendar year for any student who is determined to have brought a firearm to school. The policy may allow the chief administrative officer (as designated by the school district governing board) to modify these expulsion requirements for individual students on a case-by-case basis. (20 U.S.C., §§ 2701 *et seq.*, 3351, as amended and added by Pub. Law 103-227, §§ 1031-1032.)

The principal must also immediately suspend and recommend expulsion of a student for brandishing a knife or possession of a knife, explosive or other dangerous object at school or at a school-sponsored event off campus. (Ed. Code, § 48915, subd. (a) & (c).) Possession does not require that the offender own the weapon, have it on his or her person, or intend to use it unlawfully. Having control or the right of control over the weapon (storing it in a locker, for example) is sufficient.

Firearms

Possession of firearms, equipment and ammunition on school grounds. No one except law enforcement officers and certain other specified individuals may bring or possess any firearm, ammunition or reloaded ammunition onto public school grounds or into a "school zone" (within a distance of 1,000 feet from school grounds) without the permission of the school district superintendent or designee. (Misdemeanor or Felony, Pen. Code, § 626.9; Ops.Cal.Atty.Gen. 91 (1997).)

It is unlawful for a minor to be in possession of live ammunition unless he or she: 1) has written permission; 2) is in the presence of a parent or guardian; or 3) is going to or coming from an organized lawful recreational, shooting or hunting activity. (Misdemeanor or Felony, Pen. Code, § 12101, subd. (b).)

Possession of other prohibited firearms, equipment or ammunition. It is illegal for anyone to possess certain types of firearms, equipment or ammunition, including:

- Assault weapons. (Misdemeanor or Felony, Pen. Code, § 12280.)
- Machine guns. (Felony, Pen. Code, § 12220.)
- Short-barrel shotguns or short-barrel rifles. (Misdemeanor or Felony, Pen. Code, § 12020, subd. (a).)
- Metal military practice hand grenades and metal replica hand grenades. (Misdemeanor or Felony, Pen. Code, § 12020 subd.(a).)
- Silencers. (Felony, Pen. Code, § 12520.)
- Armor-piercing bullets. (Misdemeanor or Felony, Pen. Code, § 12320.)
- Unmarked pistols or revolvers. (Misdemeanor, Pen. Code, § 12094.)
- Sniper scopes. (Misdemeanor, Pen. Code, § 468.)

It is illegal to carry a concealed weapon in a vehicle or on one's person in a public place. Having parental permission does not affect the need for or take the place of a concealed weapons permit. (Misdemeanor or Felony, Pen. Code, § 12025.)

It is illegal to carry a loaded weapon in a vehicle or on one's person while in a public place or on any public street in prohibited unincorporated or an incorporated city area. (Misdemeanor or Felony, Pen. Code, § 12031.)

Furnishing a minor with a concealable weapon. No person, corporation, or firm shall sell, loan or transfer a firearm to a minor. (Misdemeanor or Felony, Pen. Code, § 12072 (3) (a).)

Exhibiting, drawing or using a deadly weapon or loaded firearm. It is a violation even when an unloaded or imitation fire-arm is used to "scare" a person. (Misdemeanor, Pen. Code, §§ 417, subd. (a), 417.4.) It is a felony or misdemeanor to draw a deadly weapon before a peace officer (Pen. Code, § 417, subd. (c)) and a misdemeanor or felony to draw the weapon before a reserve or auxiliary officer. (Pen. Code, § 417.1.)

Assault with a deadly weapon or loaded firearm. It is a violation for any person to commit an assault on another person with a deadly weapon or instrument, other than a firearm, or by any means of force likely to produce great bodily injury. Use of a firearm increases the penalty for such offense. (Misdemeanor or Felony, Pen. Code, § 245.)

Knives and Other Weapons

Bringing or possessing a knife, BB gun or pellet gun onto school property without authority. Possession of any knife constitutes grounds for expulsion. (Ed. Code, § 48915, subd. (a)(2).) This applies to all knives having blades longer than two and one-half inches, dirks, daggers, ice picks, folding knives with blades that lock into place, razors with unguarded blades, tasers and stun guns. (Misdemeanor or Felony, Pen. Code, § 626.10.)

Brandishing any knife or other deadly weapon. Any person who, except in self-defense, in the presence of any other person, draws or exhibits any deadly weapon whatsoever, . . . in a rude, angry, or threatening manner, or who in any manner, unlawfully uses the same in any fight or quarrel is guilty of a misdemeanor, punish-able by imprisonment in a county jail for not less than 30 days. (Misdemeanor, Pen. Code, § 417 subd. (a)(1).)

Possession, carrying, sale, lending or giving away of switchblade knives. The blade must be two inches or longer. (Misdemeanor, Pen. Code, § 653k.) (A switchblade knife resembles a pocket knife. However, the blade of a switchblade is released by flicking the wrist or pressing a button or other mechanical device, instead of being manually pulled into position.)

Possession, sale, lending or giving away of certain weapons.
The possession, sale, lending or giving away of certain weapons by any person in this state is punishable by imprisonment in a county jail not exceeding one year or in the state prison. (Misdemeanor or Felony, Pen. Code, §§ 12020, 12020, subd. (a).) The weapons are as follows:

- Blackjacks, billy clubs and slingshots.
- Metal knuckles.
- Sandclubs, saps or sandbag.
- Nunchakus.
- Throwing stars.
- Sawed-off shotguns and rifles.
- Multiburst trigger activators.
- Leaded canes.
- Concealed dagger.
- Stiletto.
- Dirk.
- Ballistic knife.
- Mechanical concealed knife or sword.
- Writing pen.
- Belt buckle.
- Lipstick case knife.

Laser pointers. Every person, except in self-defense, who aims or points a laser pointer at another person in a threatening manner with the specific intent to cause a reasonable person fear of bodily harm is in violation of the law. (Misdemeanor, Pen. Code, § 417.25.)

Reckless or malicious possession of destructive devices or explosives in or near a school. Every person who recklessly or maliciously has in his possession any destructive device or any explosive . . . in or near any school or college . . . is guilty of a felony, and shall be punishable by imprisonment in the state prison for a period of two, four, or six years. (Felony, Pen. Code, § 12303.2.)

Terrorist Acts at School

Existing law specifies that any person who explodes, ignites, or attempts to explode or ignite any destructive device or explosive, or who commits arson, in certain places such as churches, abortions clinics, libraries, courthouses, or on private property, for the purpose of terrorizing another or in reckless disregard of terrorizing another is guilty of a felony. Public or private schools providing instruction in kindergarten or grades 1 to 12 have been added to the current list of places. (Felony, Pen. Code, § 11413.)

Personal and School Property

Thefts

This section refers to the taking of personal property of another. For purposes of this section, depending upon the elements of a particular crime, a theft may be considered a misdemeanor due to the dollar value of the property involved or a felony if it was taken from the person of another regardless of value. School safety personnel need to be aware of the various dollar amounts and the circumstances under which the property was taken before taking the appropriate action. (When in doubt, contact local law enforcement or school police or security for technical assistance.) The consequences for students who violate these sections range from informal counseling to formal charges being filed in juvenile court. Consequences may also include suspension, expulsion, restitution, community service hours, fines and confinement in a juvenile lockdown facility. Theft is further defined in section 484 of the Penal Code.

Crimes Against Personal Property

Education Code section 48915, subdivision (a) requires the principal or superintendent to recommend expulsion for robbery and extortion. Other crimes such as stealing or attempting to steal property and receiving or possessing stolen property are also grounds for suspension and expulsion. (Ed. Code, §§ 48900, subds. (g) & (l).)

Grand and petty theft. Grand theft occurs when the value of stolen personal property exceeds $400, or the property — regardless of value — is taken directly from another person. (Felony, Pen. Code, §§ 487, 489.) Otherwise, it is considered petty theft. (Misdemeanor, Pen. Code, § 490.)

Theft involving computers. Unauthorized access to computers, computer systems and computer data is a crime. (Misdemeanor, Pen. Code, § 502.)

Burglary. "Every person who enters any room . . . or other building with intent to commit grand or petty larceny or any felony is guilty of burglary." (Misdemeanor or Felony, Pen. Code, §§ 459-461.)

Robbery. This crime is defined as the "felonious taking of personal property in the possession of another, from his person or immediate presence, and against his will . . . by means of force or fear." (Pen. Code, §§ 211, 213.) "Fear" may involve a threat to inflict injury to the individual or to his or her family, or to the person or property of anyone accompanying the individual being robbed. (Pen. Code, § 212.)

Example: If a student takes the shoes from the person who is carrying or wearing them by using force or fear, the act is robbery.

Example: One or more students approach Collin and demand, "Give us your lunch money or we'll beat you up." Collin then gives up his money. The students would be guilty of robbery. Usually, there is a sense of immediate danger to the victim. If Collin does not give up his money, the students are guilty of attempted robbery.

Extortion. This crime is defined as "the obtaining of property from another, with his or her consent . . . induced by a wrongful use of force or fear. . . . " (Felony, Pen. Code, §§ 518, 519, 520.) Although similar to robbery, extortion usually does not involve the same immediacy of danger to the victim.

Example: A student who demands that another student leave money in a locker and says, "If you don't, I'll get you later!" is guilty of extortion.

Receiving stolen property. A person who buys or receives property he or she knows to have been obtained through theft or extortion has received stolen property. (If the stolen property is valued at more than $400, the crime constitutes a felony; for property valued at less than $400, the crime may be reduced to a misdemeanor.) (Pen. Code, § 496.)

Possession or duplication of school keys without authorization. Any person who knowingly makes, duplicates, causes to be duplicated, or uses, or attempts to make, duplicate, causes to be duplicated, or use, or has in their possession any key of any public school without authorization is in violation. (Misdemeanor, Pen. Code, § 469.)

Failure to return lost property. There is nothing illegal about "finders keepers," as long as efforts to find the owner are sincerely made. Any item worth more than $100, however, must be turned over to law enforcement. (Misdemeanor or Felony, Pen. Code, §§ 485, 489, 490.) The finder can re-claim found property after 90 days if the owner is not located. (Civ. Code, §§ 2080-2080.3.)

Crimes Against School Property

Causing or attempting to cause damage to school or private property is grounds for suspension and expulsion. (Ed. Code, § 48900, subd. (f).)

Arson. This crime involves the act of willfully and maliciously setting fire to or causing the burning of any structure or property. It is also a crime to aid, counsel or procure materials for the burning of a structure or property. (Felony, Pen. Code, §§ 451-457.1.)

Vandalism. This crime includes the malicious defacing with graffiti or other inscribed material, damaging or destroying the real property (e.g., buildings, vehicles) or personal property (e.g., clothing) of another person. (Misdemeanor or Felony, Pen. Code, § 594.)

It is important to note that different sections of the Penal Code regarding vandalism carry varying degrees of penalties depending upon the severity of the offense. Most vandalism sections specify that if a community has adopted a graffiti abatement program, violators may be assigned to keep a specified property in the community free of graffiti for a period of 60 days to one year. A graffiti abatement program is adopted by city or county resolution and provides for the administration and financing of graffiti removal, community education on the prevention of graffiti and enforcement of graffiti laws. (Pen. Code, §§ 594, 594.1, 594.2, 594.6, 594.8.) According to Vehicle Code section 13202.6, minors 13 years of age or older who are convicted of crimes under Penal Code sections 594, 594.3 or 594.4 are required to have their driving privilege suspended or delayed for one year.

Possession of aerosol paint container, felt tip marker, drill bits or other tools with intent to commit vandalism or graffiti.
(Misdemeanor, Pen. Code, § 594.2.) Aerosol paint containers may not be: 1) purchased by a minor (Misdemeanor, Pen. Code, § 594.1, subd. (b).); or 2) possessed by a minor in a public facility where a posted sign states that it is a misdemeanor to possess such a container without authorization. (Misdemeanor, Pen. Code, § 594.1, subd. (d).) In addition, minors may not possess aerosol paint containers for the purpose of defacing property while on any street or public highway, or in any other public place. (Misdemeanor, Pen. Code, § 594.1, subd. (e)(1).)

Drug and Alcohol Offenses

Serious legal penalties are attached to the use or sale of more than 135 different substances. A small number of these substances constitute the majority of drugs reportedly used by young people. It is important for educators and parents to familiarize themselves with the symptoms of drug use and their related laws. Educators and parents should also familiarize themselves with commonly used performance enhancing drugs, and drugs used at sports events, clubs or "underground parties." School employees who learn about drug abuse will be better able to spot students who are using drugs or alcohol and take the appropriate action.[23] In many schools, students suspected of being under the influence are taken to the school nurse, resource officer or police officer for a more accurate determination of possible drug use. When apprehending such students, school officials should remember that these minors may also possess drug paraphernalia, which may be an additional criminal misdemeanor offense.

The possession, use, sale or furnishing of any controlled substance, alcohol or intoxicant (or any substance represented as an intoxicant) on school property or at a school-related activity is grounds for suspension or recommended expulsion. (Ed. Code, §§ 48900, subds. (c) & (d).) Moreover, Education Code section 48915, subdivision (a) requires the principal to recommend expulsion for the unlawful sale of any controlled substance as described above.

The principal or principal's designee must report student possession or sales of drugs to law enforcement; they may report other acts involving drugs, alcohol or other intoxicants. (Ed. Code, § 48900.) It is important for school officials and local law enforcement officials to discuss which alcohol and drug offenses must or should be reported. After deciding which cases will be processed, school and law enforcement reporting procedures should be developed, printed and distributed to all staff as part of administrative training.

School officials should not throw away confiscated drugs. All such evidence should be given to a peace officer or school safety personnel for proper storage. To maintain "chain of custody," school officials need to develop guidelines for collecting, logging and

---

[23] See the Drugs and Youth: An Information Guide for Parents and Educators booklet and *Drugs and Youth... The Challenge* video available from the Crime and Violence Prevention Center, California Attorney General's Office, P.O. Box 944255, Sacramento, CA 94244-2550 (916) 324-7863.

sealing evidence in envelopes or containers, and school personnel should be trained in their application. Their law enforcement partners can help with specific procedures for implementing these guidelines. Educators must remember that it is a misdemeanor to destroy evidence of a crime. (Pen. Code, § 135.)

Drug Offenses

Possession of paraphernalia. (Misdemeanor or Felony, Health & Saf. Code, §§ 11014.5, 11364, 11364.5, 11364.7; Ed. Code, § 48900, subd. (j).) School officials may ban all paraphernalia from campus through board action, which would then allow suspension or expulsion under the provisions of Education Code sections 48900 subdivision (j) and 35291.5.

Marijuana, hashish.

- Possession of less than 28.5 grams of marijuana, other than concentrated cannabis, on school grounds by a minor. (Misdemeanor, Health & Saf. Code, § 11357, subd. (e).)
- Possession for sale. (Felony, Health & Saf. Code, § 11359.)
- Using a minor to transport, sell or give away, or giving any amount to a minor. (Felony, Health & Saf. Code, § 11361.)
- Selling, offering to sell, transporting and importing. (Felony, Health & Saf. Code, § 11360, subd. (a).)
- Transporting or giving of 28.5 grams or less, other than concentrated cannabis. (Misdemeanor, Health & Saf. Code, § 11360, subd. (b).)
- Being under the influence. (Misdemeanor, Pen. Code, § 647, subd. (f).)

Barbiturates, LSD, PCP, amphetamines, methamphetamines.

- Possession. (Felony or Misdemeanor, Health & Saf. Code, § 11377.)
- Possession for sale. (Felony, Health & Saf. Code, §§ 11378, 11378.5.)
- Selling, presenting as a gift, transporting, furnishing, etc. (Felony, Health & Saf. Code, §§ 11379, 11379.5.)

- Involving a minor in the above crimes or furnishing barbiturates to a minor. (Felony, Health & Saf. Code, §§ 11380, 11380.5.)
- Being under the influence. (Misdemeanor, Health & Saf. Code, § 11550.)

Inhalants. (toluene or other intoxicating inhalants generally found in glue, paint, paint thinner, solvents, etc.)

- Possession of substance containing toluene or similar toxic inhalant with intent to inhale for purpose of intoxication. (Misdemeanor, Pen. Code, § 381.)
- Possession for sale, dispensing, distributing substance containing toluene or other intoxicating combination of hydrocarbons to minors except as part of a crafts kit or certified as containing a substance that makes it malodorous or induces sneezing. (Misdemeanor, Pen. Code, § 380.)
- Possession of nitrous oxide with intent to inhale for purpose of intoxication or knowingly being under the influence. (Misdemeanor, Pen. Code, § 381b.)
- Being under the influence. (Misdemeanor, Pen. Code, §§ 647, subd. (f), 381, 381b.)

Heroin, cocaine, crack cocaine.

- Possession. (Felony, Health & Saf. Code, § 11350.)
- Possession for sale. (Felony, Health & Saf. Code, § 11351.)
- Selling, presenting as a gift, transporting, furnishing, etc. (Felony, Health & Saf. Code, § 11352.)
- Involving a minor in the above crimes or furnishing these drugs to a minor. (Felony, Health & Saf. Code, §§ 11353, 11353.5, 11353.6, 11353.7, 11354.)
- Being under the influence. (Misdemeanor, Health & Saf. Code, § 11550 .)

Alcohol Offenses

Possessing, using, selling or otherwise furnishing alcohol (or a substance represented as alcohol), or being under the influence of alcohol is grounds for suspension or recommended expulsion. (Ed. Code, § 48900, subds. (c) & (d).)

- Possession, consumption, presentation as a gift, delivery or sale of alcoholic beverages on school premises (unless it meets criteria for several narrow exceptions). (Misdemeanor, Bus. & Prof. Code, § 25608.)
- Possession of alcohol by a minor. (Misdemeanor, Bus. & Prof. Code, § 25662.)
- Furnishing alcohol to a minor. (Misdemeanor, Bus. & Prof. Code, § 25658.)
- Being under the influence of alcohol. (Misdemeanor, Pen. Code, § 647, subd. (f).)

Liability of Parents and Guardians

General Liability for Injury to Person or Property

California Civil Code section 1714.1 outlines parental and guardian liability for acts of minors:

"Any acts of willful misconduct of a minor which result in injury or death to another person or in any injury to the property of another shall be imputed to the parent or guardian having custody and control of the minor for all purposes of civil damages. The parent or guardian having custody and control shall be jointly and severally liable with the minor for any damages resulting from the willful misconduct. This liability shall not exceed $25,000 for each tort of the minor, and in the case of injury to a person, imputed liability shall be further limited to medical, dental and hospital expenses incurred by the injured person, not to exceed $25,000. The liability imposed by this section is in addition to any liability now imposed by law." (Civ. Code, § 1714.1, subd. (a).)

Liability for Injury to School-Related Person or Property

California Education Code section 48904 holds the parent or guardian of any minor who causes death or injury to any student or school employee, or who damages real or personal property belonging to the district or school employees, liable for the actions of the minor, up to a sum of $20,000. This liability also applies to any school district property loaned to the minor and not returned. (Ed. Code, § 48904, subd. (a)(1).)

Liability for Computer Crime

The law defining computer crimes makes the parent or legal guardian of a minor responsible for crimes committed by the minor through the use of a computer. (Pen. Code, § 502, subd. (e)(1).)

Liability for Injury, Death or Property Damage With Firearm

When a minor under age 18 causes injury or death to another person or damages property through the discharge of a firearm, Civil Code section 1714.3 holds his or her parents or guardians responsible if they allowed the minor to have the firearm or left the firearm where it was accessible to the minor. This civil liability has a limit of $30,000 for injury to or death of one person, or $60,000 for injury to or death of more than one person in any single incident. "The liability . . . is in addition to any liability otherwise imposed by law." (Civ. Code, § 1714.3.)

Criminal Prosecution for Criminal Storage of Firearm

A parent or guardian may be prosecuted for the "criminal storage of a firearm." Prosecution of this crime requires the following to occur:

- The parent or guardian keeps a loaded firearm at a premise under his or her custody or control.
- The parent or guardian knows or reasonably should know that a child is likely to gain access to the firearm without permission.
- The child obtains access to the firearm.
- The child causes death or great bodily injury to himself, herself or another person with this firearm. (Misdemeanor or Felony, Pen. Code, § 12035.)

Additionally, new legislation provides for prosecution of persons when a juvenile gains access to a firearm and carries it off-premises. Prosecution of this crime requires the following to occur:

- The person keeps a loaded or unloaded firearm within any premise under his or her custody or control.
- The person knows or reasonably should know that a child (under 16 years of age) is likely to gain access to the firearm without permission.
- The child obtains access to the firearm.
- The child carries the firearm off-premises. (Misdemeanor, Pen. Code, § 12036.)

Juvenile Support Costs

Whenever a minor is placed in or committed to any institution, the father, mother, spouse or other person liable for the support of the minor shall be liable for the minor's reasonable support costs during placement. If the court finds that the minor committed the crime against the parent or other person supporting the minor, the parent or other person is not liable for the reasonable support costs. (Welf. & Inst. Code, § 903.)

Liability for Use of Tear Gas

Minors, who are 16 years of age, may lawfully purchase and possess tear gas if they are accompanied by a parent or guardian or have written parental permission. If a minor uses tear gas or a tear gas weapon for any purpose other than self-defense, both the student and his or her parent or guardian will be held accountable for any civil liability resulting from the incident. (Pen. Code, § 12403.8, subd. (c).)

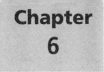
Criminal Procedures

Once school administrators, teachers, school safety personnel and staff recognize that a violation of law has occurred, it is their responsibility to take the most appropriate action necessary to minimize further incidents, stabilize and reassure the students, secure the campus and implement existing protocols addressing the particular incident.

To that end, school districts must develop written policies and procedures for conducting student searches and interviews, reporting criminal activity to law enforcement, cooperating with authorities during on-campus investigations and taking disciplinary action. Well-written guidelines inform staff, students, parents and guardians about school expectations of student conduct and the consequences of illegal activity.

This chapter outlines general procedures for handling searches and seizures, working with law enforcement, making arrests, handling suspected criminal conduct by students and addressing the problem of outsiders on campus. Better understanding of these issues will help promote a safer school environment for everyone.

Student Searches and Constitutional Standards

School officials must be familiar with the basic constitutional rights and current court opinions on student searches. Failure to comply with the reasonable suspicion and reasonable scope standards discussed below may result in the inability to use evidence in court. It may also create a liability for the searcher, school or district for violating student civil rights. (*Cales v. Howell Public Schools* (E.D.

Mich. 1985) 635 F.Supp. 454 (E.D. Mich.); *Kuehn v. Renton School District* (Wash. 1985) 694 P.2d 1078.)

The constitutional standard for student searches was set by the U.S. Supreme Court in the case, *New Jersey v. T.L.O.*, which established the reasonableness standard by which school officials may search students. In determining what is "reasonable," the student's legitimate expectation of privacy (i.e., his or her Fourth Amendment rights) must be weighed against the school's legitimate need to maintain an environment conducive to learning. The reasonableness of the search also depends on whether the action is justified at its inception, and whether the search as actually conducted is reasonably related in scope to the circumstances that justified interference in the first place. Individual states may set higher privacy criteria for their citizens than the federal constitutional guarantee, but they may not establish lower standards. (*New Jersey v. T.L.O.*, (1985) 469 U.S. 325, 83 L.Ed.2d 720, 105 S.Ct. 733.)

Reasonable Suspicion

In the landmark *William G.* case, the California Supreme Court decided that school personnel should not be held to the probable cause standard required of peace officers when determining the legality of a search. The court also ruled that a warrant is not necessary. Before searching a student, a school employee need only have a reasonable suspicion that the search will turn up evidence showing the student has engaged or is engaging in a prohibited activity. (*In Re William G.*, (1985) 40 Cal.3d 550.)

However, a search cannot be based on a mere hunch or rumor. Any suspicion must be supported by facts (e.g., information or allegations from other students that the suspect used, sold or stored illegal drugs).

In order for a court to find there was a reasonable suspicion, the judge will expect the searcher to:

- Clearly explain the reasons for his or her suspicion and the facts surrounding the incident.

- Be able to connect the student who was searched to a crime or rule violation.
- Have relied on recent, credible information from personal knowledge or observation and/or other eyewitnesses.

Reasonable suspicion may include previous similar illegal activity in that area, suspicious movements, illicit behavior or prior contacts with the student for similar illegal behavior.

Reasonable Scope

The scope of the search must also be reasonably related to the search objective and cannot be excessively intrusive in light of the student's age and sex and the nature of the offense. (*Ibid.*)

In order for a court to find that a search was reasonable in scope, the judge will expect the searcher to have:

- Intruded only to an extent that was reasonable under the circumstances to recover the contraband.
- Evaluated the seriousness of the violation when deciding how intensive the search should be.
- Considered the student's age and sex.
- Have searched only those students likely to possess evidence of the crime or rule violation.

The law requires that school searches be no more extensive than reasonably necessary. The greater the need for immediate protection of students or staff, the broader the scope of the search.

Applying Search Standards

The decision to conduct a search must be based on the facts of each individual case. Therefore, it is impossible to provide absolute, foolproof guidelines. Moreover, legal casebooks are full of cases in which the police, trial courts and appellate courts — even individual appellate justices — disagree on the legality of specific searches. (*In re Robert B.* (1985) 172 Cal.App.3d 763; *In re Corey L.* (1988) 203 Cal.App.3d 1020; *In re Bobby B.* (1985) 172 Cal.App.3d 377.)

Determining Reasonable Suspicion

Generally, the reasonable belief that a student possesses a loaded gun or dangerous drugs justifies a more intensive search, to include the student and his or her locker, bookbag, purse, desk or vehicle.

On the other hand, the loss of a small amount of money or object of minimal value would not justify as extensive a search. In one case, a police officer on school grounds detained a minor to conduct a weapons search at the explicit request of the dean of students. The officer's decision was based on information received by the dean that someone in the minor's group was reportedly in possession of a gun or other weapon. The gun accusation was made by another student during a fracas, not by an anonymous tipster. In the opinion of the appellate court judges, the danger posed by the possible possession of a weapon was more significant than the relatively minor intrusion involved in investigating the accuracy of an unidentified student's accusation. In light of the inalienable right of students to a safe, secure and peaceful campus as protected by the California Constitution, a cursory search of the minor and others in his group was not only reasonable, but constitutionally compelled. (*In re Alexander B.* (1990) 220 Cal.App.3d 1572, 1573-1574.)

However, under no circumstances should a school employee conduct a strip or body cavity search. (Ed. Code, § 49050.) The mouth is not considered a "body cavity" for these purposes. (Pen. Code, § 4030.) If the need for such an intrusive search appears warranted, school officials should seek immediate legal advice from the school attorney, district attorney or law enforcement.

In the *William G.* case, the court found that a vice principal's suspicion of student tardiness or truancy provided no reasonable basis for conducting a search of any kind. Nor did the student's attempt to conceal a calculator case with an odd-looking bulge from the vice principal by itself provide sufficient cause for a search. Moreover, the student's demand for a warrant did not create a reasonable suspicion on which to base the search. In this case, there was no information connecting this particular student or his calculator case to any illegal activity (i.e., reports from other students that the student was involved in drugs, etc.). (*Id.* at p. 567.)

In re Frederick B., a school security guard observed two students exchanging paper currency in an area on campus where he had previously caught others in drug-related acts. The Court of Appeal held that the guard had a reasonable suspicion that the minors were doing something illegal. When the guard asked the boys what they had exchanged, one student said he had given the other 50 cents. The court found that these facts justified detention in the dean's office to clear up the matter. When one of the students had to be physically restrained from leaving the area, a handgun was discovered stuck in his waistband. (The question of whether a search would have been warranted had the gun not been discovered was never litigated because possession of the handgun provided sufficient cause for arrest.) (*In re Frederick B.* (1987) 192 Cal.App.3d 79.)

In re Guillermo M., a school district security agent who knew that a student had been in trouble before and associated with a gang questioned him about the bulges in his front pant pockets, believing them to be caused by knives. The student replied that the bulges were pencils and kept walking, even after the agent asked to see the objects. The agent then stopped the student and patted him down, finding a knife in each pocket. Later that day, after being advised of his rights, the student told the police that he owned the knives. The Court of Appeal affirmed, holding that the knives and the student's later statement of ownership were admissible in evidence, since the school security agent had properly acted within the scope of his employment in detaining and patting down the student. (*In re Guillermo M.* (1982) 130 Cal.App.3d 642.)

If highly-trained judicial officers examining the same set of facts cannot agree on the reasonableness of a search done by a trained peace officer, then people untrained in the law cannot always be expected to make correct judgements. In addition, many decisions as to whether or not to conduct a search must be made quickly, during tense situations. In any case, school personnel should avoid searches for arbitrary or punitive reasons. If a decision to search is based on facts — credible, reliable information received from others, suspicious conduct, unusual odors emanating from a locker, a student's intoxicated appearance, etc. — it is likely to be upheld. The courts are generally aware of the difficult circumstances in which such decisions are made, and they take this into account when determining if a search was reasonable.

Working With Law Enforcement

A school official may form a reasonable suspicion of student wrong-doing based on information from law enforcement and then make a search with the help of peace officers. This would be considered a search by a school official, and not law enforcement, providing the official made an independent determination that a search was needed to gather evidence of student misconduct in order to protect school safety. School officials should not hesitate to ask law enforcement for assistance in obtaining information about student misconduct.

If school officials have reasonable suspicion that a student has marijuana in his pockets, they have the right to search the student. However, if the student refuses to be searched, rather than risk a violent confrontation, school officials may call a peace officer to conduct the search for them. Peace officers are professionally trained in this capacity. In conducting the search, the peace officer acts as an agent of the school official rather than in his or her own right, and the search will be upheld.[24]

On the other hand, if a school official conducts a search as a law enforcement agent rather than as an independent school official, he or she must abide by the probable cause requirements established for searches by law enforcement — not the more relaxed, reasonable suspicion standard set for school officials. The administrator is

---

[24] *In re Fred C.* (1972) 26 Cal.App.3d 320. For a more critical point of view, see *Gordon J. v. Santa Ana Unified School District* (1984) 162 Cal.App.3d 530.

acting as a law enforcement agent when he or she is requested by peace officers to conduct a search for the primary purpose of securing evidence of a criminal violation and for the purpose of making an arrest.

Students on county probation or state parole may have special conditions set by the court under which they and their possessions may be searched by law enforcement, probation or parole officers. (Welf. & Inst. Code, § 730, subd. (b); *In re Binh L.* (1992) 5 Cal.App.4th 194.) Such searches may be done from time to time to monitor student compliance with probation or parole conditions. The California Supreme Court held that an otherwise illegal search of a minor at a high school football game was not unconstitutional despite the school police officer's ignorance of a probation search condition. A juvenile probationer subject to a valid search condition cannot have a reasonable expectation of privacy over his or her personal property. (*In re Tyrell J.* (1994) 8 Cal.4th 68, 71-72, mod., *In re Tyrell J.,* 8 Cal.4th 727a (1994) and cert. den., *Tyrell J. v. California* (1995) 514 U.S. 1068.)

Educators should know which students are on probation or parole and work closely with their law enforcement supervisors. If a student on probation or parole is involved in suspected criminal activity or school rule violations, school officials should notify the probation or parole officer immediately so that appropriate action may be taken. (Ed. Code, § 48267; Welf. & Inst. Code, § 827, subd. (b).)

Conducting a Legal Search
Proper Search Protocol

Once reasonable suspicion exists to justify a search of a student, the search should always be conducted in the presence of another adult who is the same sex as the student. The student should first be asked to give up the object or to consent to the search. If he or she refuses, the student should be asked to turn pockets inside out, and the outer clothing should be patted down to feel for suspected contraband. Purses or other containers in the immediate possession of the student should be searched, in addition to lockers or vehicles, if warranted. However, the search should extend only to those areas where there is a reasonable belief that contraband will be discovered. School personnel may wish to consult with law enforcement to receive training in search techniques.

Evidence seized should be properly labeled and kept in a secure place where others have no access. Court witnesses must be able to identify the evidence as the same objects they found during their search. If weapons are involved, school officials should seek assistance from law enforcement officers, who have the necessary training and experience to conduct such a search safely.

If evidence of a crime or school rule violation is discovered, the school principal's failure to warn a student of his or her constitutional rights does not render inadmissible any evidence uncovered in a search of his or her person, or the admissions made to law enforcement officers after a student has been taken into custody. Warnings of constitutional rights are required only when questioning is initiated by law enforcement officers after a student has been taken into custody or otherwise deprived of his or her freedom of action in any significant way.

In general, questioning of a student by a principal cannot be equated with custodial interrogation by law enforcement officers. (*In re Christopher W.* (1973) 29 Cal.App.3d 777; *In re Corey L.* (1988) 203 Cal.App.3d 1020, 1021, rehg den., and review den.) Any and all statements made by students may be relayed to law enforcement or used in administrative or disciplinary hearings. It is advisable, however, to allow law enforcement officers to conduct any lengthy or extensive investigation since they are specially trained in interview techniques.

Locker Searches

It is wise for schools to have a written policy advising students and parents that lockers are school property and may be searched from time to time for health, safety or maintenance reasons. Once students know that the school retains control of lockers, they can no longer have a reasonable expectation of privacy in the lockers they use. Under these circumstances, school officials no longer need reasonable suspicion to justify locker searches.

Use of Trained Dogs for Searches

For a number of years, law enforcement, probation and school teams have relied heavily upon drug-sniffing dogs to assist them in their daily enforcement and monitoring activities. The dogs have proven to be an excellent drug deterrent strategy for supervising probationers and monitoring drug traffic in school facilities. The recent emphasis on police/probation teams housed at school sites has increased the deterrent effectiveness of the dogs.

Using dogs to detect drugs does not constitute a search. For example, in a school where a known drug problem exists, using a trained dog to sniff the air in a locker-lined corridor does not require any detention of students or search of their possessions, nor does it involve any human confrontation or invasion of legitimate privacy interests. The students' right to privacy does not cover illicit drugs; thus they cannot legitimately object to an unintrusive detection of such drugs.

Law enforcement conducted a "drug lockdown" and a random drug search of the high school parking lot. A teacher's vehicle was parked in the school's rear parking lot, unlocked and with its passenger window down. The law enforcement drug-sniffing dog alerted on the teacher's vehicle. The dog entered the vehicle and alerted on the vehicle's closed ashtray. The deputy opened the ashtray and found a partially burned, hand-rolled cigarette. The deputy conducted a field-test for marijuana, and it tested positive. The court held that the Constitution does not provide the teacher with any expectation of privacy in the odors emanating from the vehicle and the search was lawful. (*Hearn v. Board of Education* (1999) 191 F.3d 1329, 1331-1332.) A dog sniff of a person's property located in a public place is not a search within the meaning of the Fourth Amendment. (*United States v. Place* (1983) 462 U.S. 696.)

Should a dog "alert" school officials at a specific locker, they would have a reasonable suspicion to believe there is contraband inside. In this situation, examination of the locker's contents constitutes a search, but the initial use of the dog to establish reasonable suspicion for examining this particular locker would not. (*People v. Mayberry* (1982) 31 Cal.3d 335; *United States v. Place* (1983) 462 U.S. 696.) In schools where policies give students a reasonable expectation of privacy in their lockers, and in the absence of urgent circumstances or owner consent, a search warrant would be needed to open the locker and conduct a search.

Using dogs to detain students not suspected of drug possession, however, could result in the harassment and embarrassment of innocent people. If students were not permitted to leave their classrooms because school officials wanted them to be individually sniffed by narcotics dogs, for example, such tactics would intrude on student constitutional freedoms and create controversy for the school. In addition, a mistake made by a trained dog that resulted in a personal search of a student would be more intrusive and embarrassing for the student than a mistaken search of a locker. Only the most compelling situation would warrant consideration of such methods. (See *Horton v. Goose Creek Independent School District* (5th Cir. 1982) 677 F.2d 471; *Doe v. Renfrow* (1979) 475 F.Supp. 1012 modified 631 F.2d 91 (1980).)

Vehicle Searches

Any individual who drives, stops, parks or leaves standing a vehicle in the parking lot or on the grounds of any public school must have the permission of and be subject to any regulations imposed by the school district governing board. Furthermore, every school board must erect appropriate signs giving notice of any special vehicle conditions or regulations and keep a written copy of these available at the board's administrative office for anyone interested in reading them. (Veh. Code, § 21113, subds. (a) & (b).)

School district governing boards may impose a conditional vehicle search for use of the school parking lot. However, there must be a relationship between the rule and a real problem. Notice of the rule must be clearly provided to the driver so that he or she can refuse to comply by not entering the parking lot or by leaving immediately. The imposition of such a rule must be reasonable in scope.

The National School Safety Center recommends that schools install signs at every possible point of entry to a school lot. The text for the sign might read, "Vehicles Subject to Search. By entering this area, the person driving any vehicle is deemed to consent to complete search of the vehicle, all its compartments and contents, by school officials or law enforcement personnel for any reason whatsoever. This notice applies to all vehicles of any type and is in force 24 hours a day."[25]

Metal Detectors

School officials may use metal detectors to discover weapons being carried by individuals entering school property or a school-sponsored event. The detectors may be used without probable cause to believe that any particular person has a weapon.

However, an individual may not be selectively subjected to a metal detector without a particular suspicion that he or she is carrying a weapon. That is, the school may set up a system where everyone who enters is screened by the metal detector, or one where people are selected on a truly random basis. However, it would constitute harassment to selectively utilize the detector only on people with long hair or shaved heads or tattoos without additional basis for suspicion specific to these individuals. (75 Ops.Cal.Atty.Gen. 155 (1990).)

---

[25] National School Safety Center, *Student Searches and the Law,* Malibu, California: Pepperdine University, 1995

In setting up a metal detector system for screening weapons, the school should use certain safeguards to further minimize what is actually a minor intrusion. Advance written notice of the procedure should be made through letters to students and parents and/or signs that alert students before they walk past the device. In this way, a student who passes through the detector carrying a metal object does so voluntarily. If the device is activated, the student should be given the opportunity to divest himself or herself of any metal objects before a more intrusive method is used to discover them. If the activation of the metal detector is not explained satisfactorily, the use of a more comprehensive detection method such as a pat down or search of a backpack or purse is justified. However, it should be done by an employee of the same sex as the student, whose instructions should be to search only those containers that could reasonably contain a weapon. (For example, an envelope that does not contain any hard objects could not be opened.) The intrusion of a pat down search could be further minimized if conducted in a separate, private area away from the view of other students. (*Ibid.*)

Drug Testing

An Oregon school district's policy authorizing random urinalysis drug testing of students who participate in the district's athletic programs was upheld by the U.S. Supreme Court as not violating the federal Constitution's Fourth Amendment protection against unreasonable searches. However, the court cautioned against the assumption that suspicionless drug testing will readily pass constitutional muster in other contexts. The Oregon school district's policy tested only students who elected to participate in athletic programs and tested only for drugs. The program was instituted in response to an epidemic of drug use in the district, and was designed to deter drug use among school children, especially athletes, for whom the risk of harm from drugs is particularly high. (*Vernonia School Dist. 475 v. Acton* (1995) 515 U.S. 646.)

Seizures

Drugs

As previously noted, confiscated drugs should not be thrown away, but must be given to a peace officer for storage or destruction under law enforcement procedures. School officials should be provided training on evidence procedures in order to maintain "chain of custody." These should include proper collecting, logging and sealing of evidence in envelopes or containers, and securing storage prior to transfer to law enforcement. It is a misdemeanor to destroy evidence of a crime. (Pen. Code, § 135.)

Weapons

State law authorizes school personnel to take "injurious objects" from students. (Ed. Code, § 49331.) An injurious object, as specified in Penal Code sections 653 (k), 12001, 12020 and 12220, is one capable of inflicting substantial bodily damage. Possession of such an object is unnecessary for academic purposes. In addition, the object is not a personal possession or item of apparel a student would reasonably be expected to have. (Ed. Code, § 49330.)

School district policies and procedures should address the safe storage and disposition of any weapons confiscated from students. If an injurious object has been confiscated, school personnel may notify the parent or guardian. Furthermore, school officials may keep the object until the risk of its use as a weapon no longer remains, unless, during this period, the parent or guardian personally takes possession of the object. (Ed. Code, § 49332.)

If a student brings an injurious object to school and asks a certificated or classified employee to take care of it, the object may be returned to the student at the end of the day, provided it may be lawfully possessed off school grounds. (Ed. Code, § 49333.)

Detention of Students and Right to Arrest

The Right to Detain Students

As school administrators, teachers and school safety personnel provide security for a campus, it is often necessary for them to contact students to determine why they are not in class and check with all visitors to ensure that they have complied with the posted directions delineating the mandatory registration process. Therefore, detaining individuals has become a regular task for most school officials. Although most on-campus crime is committed by students, it is seldom necessary for school staff to arrest students because school personnel have ample authority to detain them. It is usually unnecessary for school officials to arrest non-students because peace officers are readily available to arrest a violator when called by school staff.

The right of school officials to exercise physical control over students is implied by the duty of teachers and administrators to "supervise at all times the conduct of children on the school grounds and to enforce those rules and regulations necessary to their protection." (*Dailey v. Los Angeles Unified School District* (1970) 2 Cal.3d 741, 747; Ed. Code, §§ 44805, 44807.) Also, the duty of school officials to hold students to "strict account" for their conduct implies the power to detain students in such locations as the administrator's office until law enforcement arrives. (Ed. Code, § 44807.)

A "teacher, vice-principal, principal or any other certificated employee of a school district, shall not be subject to criminal prosecution or criminal penalties for the exercise, during the performance of duties, of the same degree of physical control over a pupil that a parent would be legally privileged to exercise, but which in no event shall exceed the amount of physical control reasonably necessary to maintain order, protect property, or protect the health and safety of pupils, or to maintain proper and appropriate conditions conducive to learning." (Ed. Code, § 44807.)

Making Lawful Arrests

To make lawful, warrantless arrests, different requirements must be met, depending on what crime has been committed, the age of the person being arrested, the individual making the arrest, and whether or not he or she actually witnessed the crime.

Arrests by a Peace Officer

A peace officer may arrest without a warrant:

- Any person who commits a public offense in the officer's presence. (Pen. Code, § 836, subd. (a)(1).)
- Any minor who commits a misdemeanor, even if it is outside of the officer's presence. An officer may rely on the report of another person (e.g., a teacher or student) who witnessed the incident, or to whom the minor confessed, or to whom another student or staff member reported having witnessed the incident. (Welf. & Inst. Code, § 625.)
- Any person who commits an assault or battery on school grounds. (Pen. Code, § 243.5.)

In order to help relieve juvenile court criminal caseloads, law enforcement's authority has been expanded. Law enforcement is authorized to cite and release juvenile offenders charged with violations listed in Section 256 of the Welfare and Institutions Code, other than an offense involving a firearm. The violations specified are misdemeanors or other infractions (including truancy). Not only does this assist law enforcement, but this enhances and expands the role of the juvenile hearing officer. (Pen. Code, § 853.6, Welf. & Inst. Code, §§ 255, 256.)

Public officers and employees of a non-profit transit corporation may make an arrest without a warrant when the arrest is authorized by ordinance, the person making the arrest has reasonable cause to believe a misdemeanor has been committed in his or her presence, and the offense is a violation of a statute or ordinance that the officer or employee is required to enforce. (Pen. Code, § 836.5.)

Arrests by a Private Citizen

Liability. Any private citizen may make an arrest, called a private person's arrest. (Pen. Code, §§ 834, 837.) In felony cases, if the wrong person is arrested, there is no liability to the citizen making the arrest, as long as the mistake is reasonable. This is in contrast to a misdemeanor, where the right person must be arrested, and no allowance is made even for reasonable mistakes. If a citizen makes an arrest, any civil liability remains with the citizen.

Private person arrest for a misdemeanor. Any private citizen, including a teacher, administrator or student, may arrest any person for a misdemeanor under the following circumstances:

- The unlawful activity must have occurred in the presence of the person making the arrest. (*People v. Campbell* (1972) 27 Cal.App.3d 849, 854; Pen. Code, § 837.) A staff member who witnesses a criminal act may ask a teacher for help to make the arrest. If the person who does not see the crime is acting at the request of a person who did, the arrest will be lawful. (For example, if a fellow student sees James throw a rock, the student could report the incident to a teacher who did not witness it. If the teacher — acting as an assistant to the student — assists the arrest of James, the arrest will be lawful. The student has the right to arrest James; the teacher is helping the student in the arrest. (Pen. Code, § 839.)
- The activity must amount to a crime. (*Gomez v. Garcia* (1980) 112 Cal.App.3d 392.) A private person arresting someone for a misdemeanor presumes, at his or her own peril, that a crime has been committed. If the guess is wrong, the citizen can be sued for false imprisonment, no matter how much cause he or she had for believing that a crime had taken place.
- The right person must be arrested.

Private person arrest for a felony. The major difference between an arrest for a felony and a misdemeanor is that the felony must have occurred, but need not have occurred in the presence of the person making the arrest. For a felony arrest, the following two requirements must be met:

- A felony must have been committed.
- There must be reasonable cause for believing the person arrested committed the felony. (Pen. Code, § 837, subds. (2) & (3).)

Arrest Procedures

Making Arrests Quickly

Arrests should be made as soon as circumstances permit. A major reason for allowing citizens to make arrests without warrants is that they are often able to act promptly, long before law enforcement officers can arrive.

Making Statements to the Suspect

Generally, private person arrests are made: 1) while the suspect is committing or attempting to commit a crime; 2) when the suspect is immediately pursued after committing a crime; or 3) after the suspect has made a temporary escape. Under such circumstances, the law does not require a citizen to make any statements to the suspect prior to the arrest, although the suspect should be informed that he or she is under arrest. (Pen. Code, § 841.)

A suspect who wants to know why he or she is being arrested must be told the offense for which the arrest is being made. (Pen. Code, § 841.) When a citizen's arrest is not made on the spot or is made after an escape, the suspect must be informed of: 1) the intention to arrest; 2) the cause of the arrest; and 3) the authority under which the arrest is being made (i.e., that it is a private person arrest). (Pen. Code, § 841.) The cause of the arrest will be the criminal act committed, but it is not necessary for the citizen making the arrest to know the specific Penal Code section.

Use of Force During Arrest

If an arrested suspect will not come peacefully, the citizen enforcing a lawful right to arrest may use reasonable force necessary for the arrest and detention. In addition, the individual conducting the arrest may summon as many people as necessary for assistance. (Pen. Code, §§ 835, 835a, 839.) When making an arrest, no more force should be used than is necessary.

Citizens need not wait until a crime is committed to use force. A person may use reasonable force to stop a crime to prevent a public offense, or if he or she is about to be injured. (Pen. Code, §§ 692, 694.) Of course, the individual who is being lawfully arrested has no right to use force to resist the arrest. Resistance under such circumstances may itself be charged as assault or battery. (*People v. Garcia* (1969) 274 Cal.App.2d 100, 105.)

After the Arrest

After the suspect is arrested, he or she must be turned over to a peace officer without unnecessary delay or (as rarely happens) taken directly to a magistrate by the citizen making the arrest. (Pen. Code, § 847.) Usually, the person arrested is detained until law enforcement officers arrive. Before taking the suspect into custody, the officers will ask about the cause and circumstances of the arrest and request that the citizen making the arrest complete a private person's arrest form.

The rules governing the taking of confessions or admissions by law enforcement do not apply to school staff who are not peace officers or who are not acting at the direction of peace officers. (*In re Christopher W., supra,* 29 Cal.App.3d at p. 782; *In re Corey L., supra,* 203 Cal. App.3d at p. 1020.).

Accordingly, public school officials who are not classified as law enforcement officers or agents of law enforcement may question students who are arrested about suspected violations of the law or school rules without advising them of "Miranda rights." (*In re Corey L., supra,* 203 Cal.App.3d at p. 1020.) Moreover, school officials may report what a student says to law enforcement. However, statements made by the student to school staff must be voluntary — not coerced or disclosed as a result of threats.

Law Enforcement Investigations

Law enforcement officers have the right to come on campus to interview students who are suspects, witnesses to a crime or victims of suspected child abuse. Parental (or guardian) permission to interview or remove a student from school is not required. However, both law enforcement and schools should follow these suggested procedures:

- Law enforcement officers should notify school authorities before questioning a student or removing him or her from school.
- School administrators should verify the peace officer's identity and credentials, the authority under which he or she acts and the reason(s) for the student's interview or removal.
- The peace officer may request help from school officials to accomplish his or her duty. While the student is being interviewed, school officials do not have the authority or the right to be present. However, a student who is the victim of suspected child abuse shall be afforded the option of being interviewed in private or selecting any adult who is a member of the school staff, including any certificated or classified employee or volunteer aide to be present during the interview. In all other cases, the officer may, at his or her discretion, allow a school official to be present. (Pen. Code, § 11174.3.)
- If a principal or school official releases a minor child to a peace officer for removal from school, the school official must take immediate steps to notify the student's parent, guardian or responsible relative of the action and the place where the minor was taken. The only exception to this requirement is when a minor student has been taken into custody as a victim of suspected child abuse, as defined in Penal Code section 11165.6, or pursuant to Welfare and Institutions Code section 305. (Ed. Code, § 48906.)

In cases of suspected child abuse, school officials must provide the peace officer with the address and telephone number of the minor's parent or guardian. The officer must immediately notify the parent or guardian that the minor is in custody and where he or she is being held. The officer may refuse to disclose this location for up to 24 hours if he or she has a reasonable belief that such disclosure would endanger the safety or disturb the custody of the minor. However, the officer must inform the parent or guardian should the child require or receive medical or other treatment. The juvenile court must review any decision not to disclose the location where the minor is being held at a subsequent detention hearing. (Ed. Code, § 48906.) If the school receives inquiries from parents about the student's location, they should be referred to the law enforcement agency that placed the student in protective custody.

Outsiders on Campus

A chronic problem facing school officials is that of outsiders who circle the campus, loiter on school grounds or adjacent parking lots and victimize students. Such a situation could provide an ideal opportunity for students, non-students and local gang members to recruit younger members, deal drugs and intimidate students. These individuals begin "hanging out" before the school day begins and continue their activities all day — including the lunch period — until school lets out. This problem often persists because monitoring school activities and securing the campus perimeter takes time and requires many staff members.

In order to promote school safety and security for teachers, other employees, students and school property, legislation was enacted to define safe school zones and intentionally restrict access of unauthorized individuals to school grounds. (Pen. Code, §§ 626, subd. (c)(2), 627 et seq.) These laws were expanded to discourage criminal activity during school hours and at school-related events with the establishment of drug-, gang- and gun-free zones within 1,000 feet of all school campuses and 100 feet of school bus stops. (Pen. Code, §§ 627 - 627.10; Health & Saf. Code, §§ 11353.1, 11353.5,

11353.6; Pen. Code, §§ 186.22, subd. (b)(1), 626.9.) In order for safe school zones to apply, school districts need to mark each bus stop as a school bus stop. The areas described above are also considered safe school zones within 60 minutes before and after the school day, and 60 minutes before and after a school-sponsored activity.

Special Consideration: First Amendment

Under California law, minors have legitimate constitutional rights to exercise freedom of speech and expression at rallies, demonstrations and other on-campus activities where students and non-students may be present. (Pen. Code, § 627, subd. (c).) The exercise of free speech on campus by students and outsiders may not be labeled as disruptive unless there is a clear and present danger of substantial interference with school activities.

In addition, according to the law, outsiders exercising their right of free speech may not be asked to leave. If adults come to school for the purpose of handing out leaflets or talking to students about political, religious or economic matters (or other questions of public concern), they are exercising their right of free speech and may not be evicted or prosecuted as loiterers subject to the requirements set forth below. They may remain even after their supply of leaflets is exhausted in order to talk to students — even if a large group of students gather, and even if the presence of the adults causes "inconvenience, annoyance or unrest." The exercise of free speech is not an "unlawful purpose." However, in *People v. Hirst,* the court noted that activity otherwise protected by the First Amendment may be prohibited if it is carried on in such a manner as to disturb the peace or good order of the school session. (*People v. Hirst* (1973) 31 Cal.App.3d 75; *Mandel v. Municipal Court* (1969) 276 Cal.App.2d 649.)

Requirements Relating to Campus Outsiders

Registration. Schools are required to post signs at all school entrances specifying the requirement that "all outsiders who enter school grounds during school hours must register with the principal or designee." (Pen. Code, §§ 627.2, 627.6.) Registering requires outsiders to furnish their name, address, occupation, age (if under 21), purpose for visiting the school and proof of identity before entering school grounds. (Pen. Code, § 627.3.)[26]

Refusing permission to register. With the exception of those individuals specified in Penal Code 627.1 (i.e., students, parents and guardians of students, school employees and individuals whose employment requires their presence on campus, including employee union representatives on business), schools may refuse a person permission to register, or revoke registration and ask the individual to leave the campus if it reasonably appears to the school's chief administrative officer (the principal, vice-principal or designee) that the person's removal is needed to maintain order. This decision may be made if it appears that: 1) the person has entered school grounds for the purpose of committing an act likely to interfere with campus activities (Pen. Code, § 626.6); or 2) the person's presence may be disruptive to those activities regardless of his or her intent.[27] If the individual refuses to leave or returns within seven days, he or she may be fined up to $500 and jailed for up to six months. (Pen. Code, §§ 626.6, 627.7.)

Media on Campus

School administrators may place reasonable restrictions on news media members when they seek access to school grounds by requiring them to register; comply with other conditions for interviewing students, observing an event or examining the curriculum being taught; and, leave the premises if their presence would interfere with peaceful conduct of school activities. (79 Ops.Cal.Atty.Gen 58 (1996).)

---

[26] See *In re Jimi A.* (1989) 209 Cal.App.3d 482 for a discussion of school trespass laws.
[27] These sections may not be used "to impinge upon the lawful exercise of constitutionally protected rights of freedom of speech or assembly." Pen. Code, §§ 626.6, subd. (b), 627.7, subd. (b), 627.8, subd. (a).

Revoking permission to enter. The principal of a public school (or an employee designated by the principal to maintain order on campus) may also tell an outsider that permission to remain on campus has been revoked when there is "reasonable cause to believe that such person has willfully disrupted" the orderly operation of the campus. Permission to enter may be revoked for up to 14 days. (Pen. Code, § 626.4.)

Appeal rights. Any person who is denied registration or whose registration is revoked has the right to submit a written request for a hearing before the superintendent to appeal the decision. (Pen. Code, § 627.5; Ed. Code, § 32211, subd. (c).)

The appeal procedures specified in the Penal and Education Codes are somewhat inconsistent. According to Penal Code section 627.5, a person who is denied registration or whose registration is revoked may request a hearing before the superintendent in writing within five days. The hearing must be held within seven days after the principal or superintendent receives the request.

However, according to the Education Code, a person who threatens disruption or interferes with classes and is asked to leave a school may appeal to the school superintendent no later than two school days after the incident. The superintendent must render a decision within 24 hours after the appeal is made. The superintendent's decision may be appealed to the school board no later than two school days after it is rendered. The board must consider the appeal at its next scheduled public meeting. (Ed. Code, § 32211, subd. (c).)

Arresting/Prosecuting Loiterers

Loitering about any school or public place at or near where children normally congregate is a misdemeanor. (Pen. Code, § 653g.) It is not necessary that the offender be on school property to be found guilty under the law. It is sufficient that the person be loitering near the school or any place children congregate.

The difficulty with this statute is the definition of the term "loiter." The statute states that it means "to delay, to linger, or to idle about any such school or public place without lawful business for being present." While this definition sounds sufficiently broad enough to deal with any circumstances, the courts have interpreted the language to mean that someone must be lingering for the purpose of committing a crime when given the chance. (*People v. Frazier* (1970) 11 Cal.App.3d 174; *People v. Hirst, supra,* 31 Cal.App.3d at p. 75; *In re Christopher S.* (1978) 80 Cal.App.3d 903.) Under this interpretation, school authorities do not have to wait until a crime actually occurs, or for the offender to take steps toward the commission of any crime. Nor is there any need to show that an opportunity to commit a crime has occurred or might occur, or even what crime the offender might have committed if the opportunity had presented itself. It is enough that evidence exists to show the offender was lingering for the purpose of committing a crime. (*People v. Frazier, supra,* 11 Cal.App.3d at p. 174.)

The phrase "at or near campus" includes any school building, school grounds, sidewalks or streets immediately adjacent to the school. It generally includes the immediate area across the street from the school and possibly the area within the first block of the school.

It is extremely difficult to give detailed advice concerning what circumstances justify an arrest for loitering under this section. The courts have indicated that no specific evidence is necessary to justify an arrest and conviction — it must merely be apparent from "all of the circumstances" that the offender was awaiting an opportunity to commit a crime. If it appears that the "unlawful purpose" intended by the offender is to damage property or to obstruct or interfere with school operations, such entry may also be prosecuted as criminal trespass. (Misdemeanor, Pen. Code, § 602, subd. (j).)

Successful prosecution of loitering cases increases when: 1) mandated signs are posted; (Pen. Code, § 627.6.) 2) school and law enforcement agencies have carefully documented criminal activities occurring on or around school premises each time the outsider has been present; and 3) the offender has been notified that he or she is unwanted. Dates, times and specific locations where the individual has been observed on or about campus should be documented in the report, along with specific incidents involving drugs, alcohol or fights. The report should also include any possible connection between the person and suspected criminal activity, and whether he or she has been seen committing a criminal act. In some cases, it is possible to arrest a disruptive outsider — after first requesting that the individual leave — before he or she causes trouble.

Outsiders in Areas Adjacent to the School

In order for specified school officials to take specific action, such as an arrest, four conditions must be met prior to actual arrest. However, under most circumstances, when requested and properly informed of the laws, outsiders generally leave the area without incident.

As these events unfold, school officials will generally take the least restrictive method of securing their campus by simply requesting outsiders to leave the grounds. The next level is ordering outsiders to leave pursuant to Penal Code section 626.8. This section allows specified school officials to order outsiders from streets, sidewalks and public ways adjacent to the school for seven days if these individuals:

- Come onto specified property without lawful business.
- Interfere with or disrupt students or school activities.
- Remain on the property or return within seven days after being asked to leave.

In the event that the outsider does not comply, before an arrest may be made, the following four conditions must be met. First, the individual must be on school property, in a school building or upon a street, sidewalk or adjacent public way. (The individual need not be on school property when the actual arrest is made.)

Second, the individual's purpose there must be unlawful. The statute defines lawful business as any business not prohibited by statutes, ordinances or regulations. As in the loitering statute discussed earlier, a person is without lawful business only if he or she has the intent to do a prohibited act. When this statute was passed, the Legislative Counsel was of the opinion that lawful acts included:

- Minors enrolled in the school participating in non-school activities on school property (e.g., passing out political leaflets).
- Minors who are not enrolled at the school visiting school property to contact students for personal reasons (e.g., arranging social activities).
- Students enrolled at the school deciding to strike and refusing to attend class.
- Union members entering school property to contact members of the union.
- Parents entering school property to remove their child without the permission of school authorities.

Third, the individual's activities must either interfere with the peaceful conduct of the activities of the school or disrupt the school, its students or activities. Care must be used in determining that the required "disruption" is not, in fact, the unrest or noisy reaction caused by the exercise of free speech. (*In re Oscar R.*, (1984) 161 Cal.App.3d 770.)

A California Court of Appeal has held that no affirmative misconduct is necessary to constitute interference under Penal Code section 626.8. *In re Oscar R.*, a minor had been suspended from school and notified that he was not allowed on school grounds. He returned to campus on three consecutive days and was arrested on the third after having been told to leave the two previous days. The court found that his presence interfered with school activities because three school employees were required to leave their security posts to deal with the student.

Fourth, the individual must remain (or return within seven days) after being asked to leave, or must have otherwise established a "continued pattern of unauthorized entry" whether or not he or she was asked to leave. A continued pattern of unauthorized entry means that on at least two previous occasions in the same school year, the offender: 1) came onto school property or an adjacent sidewalk or public way without lawful business; 2) his or her presence was disruptive; and 3) he or she was asked to leave by the principal, principal's designee or a law enforcement or school police/security officer. (Pen. Code, § 626.8, subd. (c) (3).)

No crime has been committed unless all four conditions are met, including the condition that the outsider has either established a continued pattern of unauthorized entry, or refuses to leave or returns in seven days. (Ops.Cal.Legis. Counsel (1967) Assem.J. 5028; *In re Jimi A.* (1989) 209 Cal.App.3d 482.)

Sex Offenders

The presence of a specified registered sex offender on or around a campus represents a potential risk to students.[28] According to Penal Code section 626.8, subd. (c) (3), an administrator may ask a registered sex offender to leave without needing any evidence that the person's presence or actions are disruptive, unless he or she is the parent or guardian of a child attending the school or has written permission to be on the campus from the school's chief administrator.

Sex offenders may be arrested for establishing a continued pattern of unauthorized entry. As noted, this means that the individual came into a school or adjacent area on two previous occasions in the same school year and was asked to leave by school authorities. (Pen. Code, § 626.8, subd. (c)(4).) It is also possible to immediately arrest a specified registered sex offender for a violation of parole or probation if staying away from children is a condition of the parole or probation. Being on school grounds may be the basis for revocation of the individual's parole or probation. (Pen. Code, §§ 3060, 1203 et seq.)

---

[28] See Penal Code section 290, subdivision (a) for definition of "sex offender."

The DOJ, Bureau of Criminal Information and Analysis, provides information to the general public on registered sex offenders. Anyone having a reasonable suspicion that a child may be at risk from a sex offender may call 1-900-448-3000. The caller should be prepared to identify himself or herself and provide the following information about the individual they are concerned about: 1) his or her name; and 2) his or her address, date of birth, social security number or California driver's license number. If the above information is not available, the caller will need to provide the person's name and at least five of the following identifiers: height, weight, hair color, ethnicity/race, or description of scars, tattoos or birthmarks. The request will cost $10 per call for information on two people. The caller's phone number will be recorded and charged automatically.

In 1996, California enacted "Megan's Law," which provides the public with photographs and descriptive information on serious sex offenders residing in California. Megan's Law is named after seven-year old Megan Kanka, a New Jersey girl who was raped and killed by a known child molester who had moved in across the street from the Kankas — without their knowledge. In 1996, the Kankas testified in front of the California Legislature on behalf of a bill drafted and sponsored by DOJ. Ultimately, AB 1562 (Alby) was passed by the Legislature and signed by the Governor on September 25, 1996. The legislation amended Sections 290 and 290.4 of the Penal Code. Megan's Law increases public safety through community notification of registered sex offenders.

Since July 1, 1997, the public has been able to visit their local sheriff's offices and numerous police departments to view a CD-ROM computer disk. As of July 14, 2000, the CD-ROM lists over 70,600 registered serious sex offenders and over 1,555 high-risk sex offenders in California. Other sex offenders are required to register, but are not subject to disclosure under Megan's Law. These other sex offenders are individuals convicted of pornography, exhibitionism, misdemeanor sexual battery, incest or spousal rape. Additionally, sex offenders adjudicated in juvenile court are not subject to public disclosure. As of July 14, 2000, there were over 13,815 "other" registered sex offenders. DOJ updates the CD-ROM four times annually. The CD-ROM provides information searches by name, physical description, county or zip code. Approximately half of the registered serious sex offenders and more than 80% of the high-risk entries have photographs attached.

These offenders have been convicted of committing sex crimes and are required to register their whereabouts with local law enforcement. In order to view the CD-Rom, interested parties must: be at least 18 years of age or older and provide a California driver's license or identification card. They must also sign a statement that they are not a registered sex offender; that they understand the purpose for releasing the information is to protect the public — especially children — from sex offenders and that it is illegal to use the information to harass, discriminate or commit a crime against any registrant. Those who wish to view the CD-ROM may also need to state a distinct purpose for doing so, if required by local law enforcement.

In addition to providing citizens with information regarding registered sex offenders, Megan's Law provides law enforcement with three different methods to notify the public if they are under potential threat by a registered serious sex offender. The methods are:

1) While on patrol, officers may notify individuals that s/he deems to be at risk if they are in proximity to a registered serious sex offender.
2) Local police may also warn residents, schools, churches or any other community members at risk that a registered serious sex offender resides nearby.
3) For high-risk offenders, law enforcement may literally advertise, in any manner they see fit, to the community they protect and reveal the identity and whereabouts of the offender.

Drug Offenders

In 1994, California lawmakers enacted legislation to deter drug offenders from being on or near school grounds. According to the law, specified drug offenders who: 1) enter a school building, school grounds or adjacent sidewalk or public way; and 2) remain there, re-enter or otherwise establish a continued pattern of unauthorized entry within seven days of being asked to leave by designated school officials or public safety officers, are guilty of a misdemeanor. As noted, a continued pattern of unauthorized entry means that the individual came into a school or adjacent area on two previous occasions in the same school year and was asked to leave by school authorities. (Pen. Code, § 626.85, subd. (c)(2).)

Other Adults

If First Amendment considerations are not at issue, any minor over 16 years of age or adult who disrupts classes or extracurricular activities or creates substantial disorder in a location where school employees are performing their duties is guilty of a misdemeanor. (Ed. Code, § 44811.)

Arresting Former Students, Non-Students or Employees and Other Outsiders

A student suspended or expelled for disruptive behavior or a terminated employee may attempt to spend his or her new-found free time on campus, causing more trouble. The following criminal statutes will help school staff work in tandem with local law enforcement or school district police and security departments to remove these individuals from campus.

Unauthorized Campus Entry

Any student or employee who, after a hearing, has been suspended or dismissed from a school for disrupting orderly campus operations and notified by registered mail of denied access to campus may be charged with a misdemeanor for willfully and knowingly entering the campus without the express written permission of the school's chief administrative officer (the principal, vice-principal or designee). (Pen. Code, § 626.2.)

Trespassing

Refusing to leave a public agency building at any time when the building is regularly closed to the public and when asked to do so by a security guard or custodian of the building is a misdemeanor. (Misdemeanor, Pen. Code, § 602, subd. (p).)

Damaging Property/Interfering With Business

It is also a crime to enter a public agency building for the purpose of damaging property or disrupting normal business transactions. (Misdemeanor, Pen. Code, § 602, subd. (j).)

Interfering With School Classes or Activities

Any minor over 16 years of age or adult who is not a student at the school, including any minor or adult parent or guardian of a student at the school, is prohibited from entering school grounds or buildings and willfully interfering with the "discipline, good order, lawful conduct, or administration of any school class or activity . . . with the intent to disrupt, obstruct, or to inflict damage to property or bodily injury upon any person." (Ed. Code, §§ 44810, 44811.) (See also *In re Christopher S.* (1978) 80 Cal.App.3d 903.)

Reporting School Crime

Under the California Safe Schools Assessment (CSSA) Program, every school district and county office of education is required to report crime on school campuses to the California Department of Education or its designee on a semiannual basis. (Pen. Code, §§ 628-628.6.) The purpose of the school crime reporting program is to obtain accurate data and information about the type and frequency of crime occurring on school campuses.[29] This information helps

---

[29] For more information on how and what to report or any other related crime reporting questions, contact the California Safe Schools Assessment Program at (800) 273-6363 or their web site: http://www.cssa.butte.k12.ca.us. See also *Understanding and Reporting School Crime, California Safe Schools Assessment,* c/o Butte County Office of Education, 1859 Bird Street, Oroville, CA 95965.

facilitate the development of effective programs and techniques to deter school crime. (Pen. Code, §§ 628 *et seq.*)

Failure to report school crime or submission of intentionally misleading data may result in withholding of an amount equal to the superintendent's salary from the district's next state funding apportionment by the Superintendent of Public Instruction until an accurate report is filed. (Ed. Code, § 14044.)

The requirement that teachers and administrators report certain types of crimes should be viewed as beneficial rather than negative. A high incidence of campus violence does not necessarily indicate poor school leadership or incompetent staff, but may merely reflect surrounding community problems.

The Department of Education is required to annually distribute (upon request) to each county office of education, school district governing board, probation department and sheriff's department a summary of that county's school district crime reports and county crime reports. This information shall be supplied no later than March 1 of each year for the previous school year. The department shall also submit to the Legislature a summary of the statewide aggregated data no later than March 1 of each year for the previous school year. Additionally, commencing with the second annual report, the department shall identify trends in school crime and evaluate school district and county school crime prevention programs by comparing the numbers and rates of crimes and the resulting economic losses for each year against those of previous years. (Pen. Code, § 628.2.)

All school district, county and statewide reports prepared under this chapter shall be deemed public documents and shall be made available to the public at a price not to exceed the actual cost of duplication and distribution. (Pen. Code, § 628.2.)

A site, district or county school crime report can also be used as a training tool to help personnel distinguish between criminal acts and disciplinary problems, identify campus crime trends, properly report student crimes and devise future crime prevention methods. The CSSA Program conducts regular training sessions on recognizing crime and reporting procedures. Representatives from the School/ Law Enforcement Partnership Program, law enforcement agencies and probation departments can also provide training to school staff on recognizing, reporting and reducing school crime.

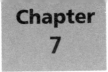

Interagency Collaboration, Confidentiality Laws and Information Sharing

This chapter focuses on interagency collaboration and the importance of information sharing between safe schools partners.

Schools will be more likely to succeed if school safety concerns are approached from an interagency perspective. Cooperation among parents, educators, students, law enforcement, courts, probation departments, youth-serving agencies and private citizens working together significantly prevents and reduces violence in schools.

Interagency Collaboration

Interagency collaboration is a mechanism for identifying, coordinating and utilizing human and financial resources from a variety of community agencies. Through interagency collaboration, people and agencies work together toward a common goal. They share information, resources and ideas. Interagency collaboration coordinates public and private resources from programs whose objectives are similar or complimentary. Because successful transition requires a breadth of experience, a team approach to preparation and planning is important. This team approach requires individuals from various backgrounds to come together and collaborate to solve problems.[30]

---

[30] *Interagency Collaboration: Making Meaningful Connections.* Originally published in 1996 under a grant from the U.S. Department of Education, through the Maine Department of Education to the Muskie School for Public Service (Institute for Disability Policy), University of Southern Maine (1995)

Once interagency collaboration truly exists, the benefits are many. Bureaucratic red tape diminishes, strong partnerships develop and services can be coordinated, thereby reducing duplication of effort and making programs more cost effective. Educators and law enforcement have modeled the interagency collaboration process, as exemplified by safe school planning; police and probation teams on campuses; school police and security departments; SARBs; child abuse multidisciplinary teams (Welf. & Inst. Code, § 830.1.); truancy-mediation, stay-in-school and diversion programs; and Healthy Start. The beneficiaries of these collaborations have been students.

More than ever, dedicated school resource officers, juvenile specialists and school police officers are involved in collaborative relationships, working with youth, educators, parents and administrators before a crisis occurs. Today's law enforcement and probation officers are as deeply committed as school personnel to counseling young offenders and determining appropriate actions. They regularly receive specialized training on child and adolescent development, assessing root causes of delinquent behavior and intervention techniques. The officers share common concerns with school administrators — enhanced student welfare, safe school environments and secure communities. These universal goals represent the foundation for mutually supportive relationships.

Schools which embrace the presence of police officers, deputy sheriffs and probation officers on campus and offer office space even for brief visits are generally safe environments. When school staff, law enforcement, courts, probation officers and child protective services staff work closely together, team relationships develop, credibility is established and the organizations usually function well as a team before, during and after a crisis situation. Ultimately, each agency better understands the goals of the others and appreciates alternative perspectives and needs.

School officials regularly seek out and invite law enforcement representatives to be guest speakers, serve as campus safety and discipline committee members and provide input into other school-related committees. Educators realize that the presence of law enforcement on campus should not be limited strictly to crisis situations or enforcement roles, but should also include positive community events such as career days and special citizenship awards ceremonies.

It is not unusual for sheriffs and police chiefs to assign deputy sheriffs and peace officers as school resource/liaison officers. These representatives may be housed within a centralized school resource center site along with juvenile probation, social services and at-risk youth intervention services. School administrators may have officers establish specific hours for meeting and counseling students. Additionally, officers may be scheduled for classroom teaching. Schools benefit from these arrangements because campus-situated officers know their school's dynamics and can respond more quickly to on-site incidents.

Local education agencies and their law enforcement partners have several options when applying for state and federal funding to bring law enforcement onto their campuses. The School Community Policing Partnership Act of 1998 established a competitive grant program. (Ed. Code, §§ 32296-32296.5.) Local education agencies and their law enforcement partners may apply, through the School/ Law Enforcement Partnership Program, for funding to implement or expand a school community policing approach to deal with school crime and safety issues.[31] Additionally, law enforcement may apply directly to the U.S. Department of Justice, Community Oriented Policing Services, School-Based Partnership Program (SBP). The SBP grant provides police agencies the unique opportunity to work with schools and community-based organizations to address persistent school-related crime problems. All applicants are required to focus on one primary school-related crime or disorder problem, occurring in or around an elementary or secondary school.[32]

---

[31] Refer to http://www.cde.ca.gov/spbranch/safety/grant_page.html for complete grant details.
[32] Refer to http://www.usdoj.gov/cops/gpa/grant_prog/sbp/default.html for more complete grant details.

Parents must not and should not be excluded from the collaborative process. Section 51101 was added to the Education Code in 1999. This section is often referred to as the "Parent's Bill of Rights." This section requires governing boards of school districts to adopt a policy developed jointly with parents and guardians that outlines a comprehensive partnership and working relationship that is mutually supportive and respectful. Furthermore, this section provides that parents and guardians of pupils enrolled in public education have the right to be informed by the school of their children's progress, and participate in the education of their children.

Interagency Problem Solving

Interagency partners may have different official priorities when addressing school and community safety issues. However, these different priorities should not preclude them from working together. For example, the first priority of law enforcement concerns public safety. The primary goal for protective services is shielding children from abuse and neglect. The objective of the school is educating young people. When the partners work jointly to create safe schools, they realize how their separate priorities mesh.

Interagency approaches to broad issues such as school safety take time and commitment. The complex, multidimensional problems involved in creating a safe school environment require the collective minds and energies of school administrators, law enforcement and probation officers, child protective services personnel and private citizens. No one agency acting alone has adequate resources to effectively deal with violence and its related problems, but collectively, participating organizations can overcome barriers and resolve issues.

Establishing partnerships between schools, government and public/ private community agencies is good business. It improves communication between systems and strengthens the possibilities of increasing school safety. Schools, law enforcement, district attorneys' offices, probation departments and child protective services agencies should convene regular meetings to discuss school safety strategies and resolve mutual concerns.

These interagency problem-solving sessions may result in the implementation of strategies for:

- Providing school liaison officers.
- Cross-training school employees on search and seizure issues.
- Instituting zero tolerance policies and identifying alternative placements.
- Establishing written protocols between law enforcement, probation and child protective services investigators.
- Developing truancy prevention strategies and crisis management plans for campus incidents (suicide, shooting, major injury, etc.).
- Organizing school community violence prevention action teams and community volunteer campus security programs.
- Facilitating the transfer of student information for appropriate educational placements.
- Training staff to recognize child abuse and comply with mandatory reporting requirements and procedures.

Exchange of Information

The ability of schools and law enforcement to freely share confidential information is critical to their success. The most pertinent Welfare and Institution, Penal and Education Code sections relating to the exchange of information between agencies are highlighted in this chapter.

As always, when dealing with confidential juvenile information, all interested parties must keep in mind the various statutes and interagency agreements which may restrict and control the dissemination and sharing of specific information.

One especially important consideration with regard to privacy interests is the Federal Educational Rights and Privacy Act (FERPA). This act is a complex federal law that protects the privacy interests of parents and students regarding education records. It affects every public elementary and secondary school and virtually every post secondary institution in the country. Congress has amended FERPA seven times with the most recent in 1994 through the Improving America's Schools Act.

In June 1997, the U.S. Department of Justice and U.S. Department of Education published a program report, *Sharing Information: A Guide to the Family Educational Rights and Privacy Act and Participation in Juvenile Justice Programs.*[33] This guide is for educators, law enforcement personnel, juvenile justice professionals and community leaders who are interested in developing interagency information sharing agreements.

In 1994, the Legislature reaffirmed its general belief that juvenile court records should be confidential, although it provided schools access to juvenile court documents. Lawmakers sought to ensure the rehabilitation of juvenile criminal offenders and decrease potential drug use, violence and other forms of delinquency by promoting more effective communication among juvenile courts, law enforcement agencies and schools. (Welf. & Inst. Code, § 827, subd. (a).)

Juvenile law enforcement records may be shared with other law enforcement agencies or any person or agency with a legitimate need for the information for official disposition of a case. (Welf. & Inst. Code, § 828.) Availability of school records is governed by the federal Family Educational Right to Privacy Act.

Any records or reports prepared or released by a court, probation department or county department of social services, or any portion of these documents, must not be released by the receiving agencies to any individuals or agencies other than those authorized to receive such documents. (Welf. & Inst. Code, § 827, subd. (a).)

---

[33] *Sharing Information: A Guide to the Family Educational Rights and Privacy Act and Participation in Juvenile Justice Programs,* is available from the U.S. Department of Justice, Office of Juvenile Justice and Delinquency Prevention, 633 Indiana Avenue, NW, Washington, D.C. 20531.

In 1994, the Legislature also authorized members of a juvenile justice multidisciplinary team to disclose and exchange non-privileged information and writings. The term "multidisciplinary team," applies to any group of three or more individuals who are trained in the prevention, identification and control of juvenile crime, including, but not limited to, criminal street gang activity, and qualified to provide a wide range of services related to problems posed by juvenile crime and criminal street gangs. The team may include school district personnel with experience or training in juvenile crime or criminal street gang control. (Welf. & Inst. Code, § 830.1.)

Team members who receive information from juvenile records have the same obligation regarding privacy and confidentiality as the person providing the data and must maintain it in a manner that ensures confidentiality. (*Ibid.*)

Exchange of Information for Certain Crimes

If a minor has been taken into court for allegedly committing a crime against property, students or school district personnel, or has been found guilty of such a crime by the juvenile court, information about the offense may be exchanged by law enforcement, the school district superintendent and the student's principal. (Welf. & Inst. Code, § 828.3.)

Access to Student Records

There are circumstances in which law enforcement agencies need access to information contained in student records. The most common way to obtain juvenile records is to have the minor and his or her parent or guardian sign a written consent. (Ed. Code, § 49075.) Schools and probation, social services, parole agencies and other organizations have used these consent or waiver forms successfully for years. Most parents and guardians want to cooperate in the service plan for their child; therefore, it is rare for anyone to refuse to sign such a waiver.

Another easy way to legally share records is to obtain a general order from the juvenile court that authorizes interagency record sharing. Juvenile court judges have discretion to issue such orders (commonly known as TNG orders) releasing juvenile court, school and other agency records to appropriate agencies for governmental purposes. (*TNG v. Superior Court* (1971) 4 Cal.3d 767.) Each county juvenile court should have a TNG order on file, so that school staff can obtain a copy. The order should be modified, if necessary, to include all interagency partners working on school safety issues. The court is interested in promoting public safety, helping the juvenile justice system function efficiently and making its own decisions with the best information available.

In 1996, school districts and county education offices were authorized to participate in an interagency data information system that permits access to a computer database system within and between government agencies or districts. Cities and counties were also authorized to establish computerized data base systems that allow law enforcement agencies, probation departments and school districts access to law enforcement, probation, school and juvenile court information and records. (Ed. Code, § 49076, subd. (c); Welf. & Inst. Code, § 827.1, subd. (a).)

Another point of access to student records for law enforcement is through information from the school district's student directory. However, in order to protect student privacy, no information can be accessed regarding any student when a parent has notified the school district that such information must not be released. (Ed. Code, § 49073.)

Emergency Information

In order to protect student health and welfare, a school district governing board may require parents or guardians to furnish information that will be kept on file at school in case of an emergency. The information should include: 1) the student's current home address and telephone number; 2) the business address and telephone number of the parent or guardian; and 3) the name, address and telephone number of a relative or friend authorized to take care of the student in an emergency situation if the parent or guardian cannot be reached. (Ed. Code, § 49408.)

Recovery of Abducted Children

All state, county and local agencies must cooperate with the district attorney regarding the location, seizure and recovery of abducted, concealed or detained minor children, as specified in Family Code Division 8, Part 2, Chapter 8, beginning with section 3130. (Welf. & Inst. Code, § 11478.)

When student records are requested by law enforcement, there must be a "proper police purpose" for use of the information. This means there must be probable cause that the student has been kidnaped, and that his or her abductor may have enrolled the student in a school, prompting the agency to begin an active investigation. In addition, the request for student information must meet the following requirements:

- The information may only be requested and received by designated peace officers, federal criminal investigators and federal law enforcement officers whose names have been submitted to the school district in writing by a law enforcement agency. The agency must ensure that school districts have an updated list of the officers who are authorized to request information.
- Designated peace officers may obtain only student record information authorized by the Education Code.
- The law enforcement agency requesting student records cannot use or disclose the information for any purpose other than to investigate the suspected kidnaping. Violation of this stipulation is punishable as a misdemeanor.
- A record of the requested information must be kept on file by the agency, including the name of the student, consent of his or her parent or guardian, officer making the inquiry, school district, district employee to whom the request was made and information requested.

- All requests for information not made to the school district in writing must be confirmed in writing before any information is released. (Ed. Code, § 49076.5.)

School districts, officials and employees are not subject to criminal or civil liability for releasing student record information in good faith as authorized by the Education Code. (*Ibid.*)

Missing Children: Posting of Information and Investigation

Public primary schools shall post at an appropriate area, restricted to adults, information regarding missing children provided by DOJ. Public secondary schools shall also post at an appropriate area information regarding missing children provided by DOJ. (Pen. Code, § 14208; Ed. Code, § 38139.)

Upon the initial enrollment of a pupil in a public or private elementary school, the school principal is urged to check to see if the child resembles a child listed as missing by the bulletins provided by DOJ pursuant to Section 14201 of the Penal Code. (Ed. Code, § 49068.5.)

Any law enforcement agency responsible for the investigation of a missing child shall inform the school district, other local educational agency or private school, in which the child is enrolled, that the child is missing. The notice shall be in writing, shall include a photograph of the child if a photograph is available and shall be given within ten days of the child's disappearance. For public schools this shall be in addition to the posting requirements set forth in Section 38139 above. Schools shall then place a notice that the child has been reported missing on the front of each missing child's school record. If a school receives a record inquiry or request from any person or entity for a missing child about whom the school has been notified pursuant to this section, the school shall immediately notify the law enforcement authorities who informed the school of the missing child's status. (Ed. Code, § 49068.6.)

Disclosure of Minor's Name for Felony Offenses

The name of a minor 14 years of age or older who has committed a specified, serious felony offense may be disclosed to the public once a juvenile court has declared that he or she is a ward based on the commission of that crime. (Welf. & Inst. Code, § 204.5.)

Law enforcement agencies may disclose the name of any minor 14 years of age or older taken into custody for committing a serious felony if a hearing has been held based on an allegation that the minor has committed a crime (i.e., the minor is a penal code offender as described in Welfare and Institutions Code section 602.) (Welf. & Inst. Code, § 827.5.)

The presiding juvenile court judge may authorize a law enforcement agency to disclose the name and other information necessary to identify a minor who is lawfully sought for arrest as a suspect in the commission of any felony listed in subdivision (b) of Welfare and Institution Code section 707 where the disclosure is imperative for the apprehension of the minor. In deciding whether to authorize the release of this information, the court must balance the confidentiality interests of the minor, the due diligence of law enforcement in trying to apprehend the minor and public safety. When seeking a court order under this section, a law enforcement agency must submit a declaration and supporting exhibits showing the probable cause for the arrest of the minor, efforts to locate the minor and why the court order is critical (e.g., the minor's danger to himself/herself or others, flight risk and any other information indicating the urgency for a court order). (Welf. & Inst. Code, § 827.6.)

In addition, law enforcement is authorized to release the name of, and any descriptive information about, a minor, 14 years of age or older, and the offenses allegedly committed by that minor, if there is an outstanding warrant for the arrest of that minor for an offense described in paragraph (1) of subdivision (e) of Welfare and Institution Code section 707 (murder where the minor personally killed the victim). Any releases made pursuant to this section shall be reported to the presiding juvenile court judge. (Welf. & Inst. Code, § 828.01.)

Court Orders

School districts are authorized to furnish information concerning a student in response to a subpoena as well as a court order. The school district must make a "reasonable effort" to notify the student and his or her parent or guardian "in advance of such compliance if lawfully possible within the requirements of the judicial order." (Ed. Code, § 49077.)

Subpoenas

If a public school employee is served with a subpoena for the purpose of furnishing a student school record, the employee may appear in person or submit a copy of the record to the court or other agency issuing the subpoena and the proper time and place. The copy must be accompanied by an affidavit certifying that it is a true copy of the original record on file at the school. (Ed. Code, § 49078.)

Petition to Seal Juvenile Records

A person who commits a misdemeanor while under the age of 18 years may petition the court for an order sealing the record of the conviction and other official case records. This order may include records of arrests that resulted in the criminal proceeding and records relating to other offenses charged in the pleading, or whether the defendant was acquitted or charges were dismissed. If the court finds that the person was under 18 at the time, it may issue an order to seal the records. After the records are sealed, the conviction, arrest or other proceeding will not have officially occurred, and the petitioner may answer any question regarding these events (e.g., when filling out a job application) as though they had not taken place. (Pen. Code, § 1203.45.) The court shall not order the records sealed in any case unless the petition indicates that there is no pending civil litigation directly relating to, or arising from, the criminal act that caused the records to be created. However, once the civil case is closed, the records may be sealed. (Welf. & Inst. Code, § 781 (a).)

Any minor who has been cited to appear before a probation officer, has been taken before a probation officer pursuant to Section 626 or has been taken before any officer of a law enforcement agency, and no accusatory pleading or petition to adjudge the minor a ward of the court has been filed, the minor may request in writing that the law enforcement agency and probation officer having jurisdiction over the offense destroy their records of the arrest or citation. (Welf. & Inst. Code § 781.5(a).)

If the court finds a minor factually innocent of the charges for which the arrest was made or the citation was issued, then the court shall order the law enforcement agency and probation officer having jurisdiction over the offense, DOJ and any law enforcement agency or probation officer that arrested or cited the minor or participated in the arrest or citation of the minor for an offense for which the minor has been found factually innocent under this section, to seal their records relating to the minor and the court order to seal and destroy those records, for three years from the date of the arrest or citation and thereafter to destroy those records and the court order to seal and destroy those records. (Welf. & Inst. Code § 781.5(c).)

Additionally, any minor who has been arrested or for whom a citation has been issued, and an accusatory pleading or petition to adjudge the minor a ward of the court has been filed, but not sustained, the minor may, at any time after dismissal of the proceeding, request in writing from the court that dismissed the proceeding a finding that the minor is factually innocent of the charges for which the arrest was made or the citation was issued. (Welf. & Inst. Code, § 781.5.(d).)

Written Notice of Felony or Misdemeanor to Superintendent

The court must provide written notice within seven days to the district superintendent that a minor enrolled in a public school has been found to have committed any felony or misdemeanor involving curfew, gambling, alcohol, drugs, tobacco products, carrying of weapons, a sex offense listed in Penal Code section 290, assault or battery, larceny, vandalism or graffiti. The written notice must only include the offense for which the minor was convicted and the disposition of the case. (Welf. & Inst. Code, § 827, subd. (b)(2).)

The district superintendent is required to "expeditiously transmit" this information to the appropriate school principal. The principal must "expeditiously disseminate" the information to those counselors who are responsible for directly supervising or submitting reports on the student's behavior or progress. In addition, the principal may make the information available to any teacher or administrator with similar responsibilities if the principal believes these individuals need the information in order to effectively work with the student or to avoid being potentially victimized. (*Ibid.*)

Any such information received by a teacher, counselor or administrator is confidential "for the limited purpose of rehabilitating the minor and protecting students and staff." It must not be further disclosed other than for necessary communication with the minor, his or her parents or guardians, law enforcement personnel or the student's probation officer, either to bring about the minor's rehabilitation or protect students and staff. Intentionally violating these confidentiality provisions is a misdemeanor punishable by a fine of up to $500. (*Ibid.*)

Duty to Inform Teachers of Student Criminal Offenses

School districts are required to inform the teacher about any student who has engaged in (or is reasonably suspected of having engaged in) any of the acts described in Education Code section 48900, except for smoking. Information must be provided to the teacher from any records customarily maintained by the district or received from a law enforcement agency. (Ed. Code, § 49079, subd. (a).) "No school district, or its officer or employee, shall be civilly or criminally liable for providing this information unless it is proven that the information was false and that the district or its officer or employee knew that the information was false, or was made with a reckless disregard for the truth or falsity of the information provided." (Ed. Code, § 49076, subd. (b).)

Any school district officer or employee who "knowingly fails to provide information" about a student who has engaged in (or is reasonably suspected of having engaged in) any of the acts described in Education Code section 48900, except for smoking, is guilty of a misdemeanor punishable by a county jail sentence of up to six months, or by a fine of up to $1,000, or both. (Ed. Code, § 49079, subd. (c).) A teacher who is given information about a student according to the provisions of Education Code 49079 must receive it "in confidence for the limited purpose for which it was provided" and cannot further disclose the information. (Ed. Code, § 49079, subd. (e).)

Value of Information Sharing

Public policy leaders, including many educators, are recognizing the value of sharing as much information as possible between professionals who are responsible for student and school safety. The policy trend is leaning toward a more open criminal/behavioral record system, even for juveniles, and establishing local procedures to prepare for this possibility begins with the concept of interagency collaboration.

Selected Resources

This list is arranged in four sections: Victims Services, Internet Web Sites, Publications and Videos.

Victims Services

California Attorney General
Office of Victims' Services
1300 I Street
Sacramento, CA 95814
(916) 324-5035 or
1-877-433-9069

Victim's Legal Resource Center
McGeorge School of Law
3200 Fifth Avenue
Sacramento, CA 95817
(916) 739-7049 or
1-800-842-8467

State Board of Control
Victims of Crime Program
P.O. Box 3036
Sacramento, CA 95812-3036
(916) 322-4426 or
1-800-777-9229
www.boc.cahwnet.gov/VICTIMS.htm

Office of Criminal Justice Planning
Victims Services/Violence Prevention
Division
1130 K Street, Suite 300
Sacramento, CA 95814
(916) 324-9128
www.ocjp.ca.gov/

California Youth Authority
4241 Williamsbourgh Drive
Sacramento, CA 95823
(916) 262-1392
http://www.cya.ca.gov/organization/
opvs/info.html

Internet Web Sites

Attorney General Bill Lockyer
Crime and Violence
Prevention Center
http://caag.state.ca.us/cvpc

California Department of Justice
http://caag.state.ca.us

California Attorney General's
Office: Opinions Unit
http://caag.state.ca.us./opinions

John Burton's Cyberspace
http://www.fontana.K12.ca.us/burton

Safe Schools and Violence
Prevention Office
http://www.cde.ca.gov/spbranch/safety/

School/Law Enforcement
Partnership Program
http://www.cde.ca.gov/safety/
partnership.html

National Criminal Justice
Information Center
http://www.ncjrs.org/

California Legislative Information
http://www.leginfo.ca.gov

California Codes
http://www.leginfo.ca.gov/calaw.html

California State PTA
http://www.capta.org/

California School Boards Association
http://www.csba.org/

National Association of Attorneys
General and the National School
Boards Association
http://www.keepschoolssafe.org/

U.S. Department of Education
http://search.ed.gov/

Publications

California Laws Relating to Minors
Legal Books Distributing
4247 Whiteside Street
Los Angeles, CA 90063
(323) 526-7110
(323) 526-7112 (FAX)
www.discovery-press.com

*Child Abuse: Educator's
  Responsibilities*
Child Abuse Prevention Handbook
*Drugs and Youth: An Information
  Guide for Parents and Educators*
Office of the Attorney General
Crime and Violence Prevention Center
P.O. Box 94244-2550
Sacramento, CA 94244-2550
(916) 324-7863
www.caag.state.ca.us/cvpc

*The California Peace Officers
  Legal Sourcebook*
Department of General Services
Publications Section
4675 Watt Avenue
North Highlands, CA 95660
(916) 928-4630
www.pd.dgs.ca.gov

*Safe Schools: A Handbook for
  Violence Prevention*
National School Safety Center
National Educational Service
P.O. Box 8
1610 W. Third Street
Bloomington, IN 47402
(812) 336-7700
(812) 336-7790 (FAX)
www.nesonline.com

*Safe Schools: A Planning Guide
  for Action*
*School Attendance Review Boards
  Handbook, Operations and
  Resources*
California Department of Education
Bureau of Publications, Sales Unit
P.O. Box 271
Sacramento, CA 95812-0271
(916) 323-2183
www.cde.ca.gov

Student Searches and the Law
National School Safety Center
Pepperdine University
Malibu, CA 90265
(805) 373-9977
(805) 373-9277 (FAX)
www.nssc1.org

Videos

Available through:
Office of the Attorney General
Crime and Violence Prevention Center
P.O. Box 94244-2550
Sacramento, CA 94244-2550
(916) 324-7863
www.caag.state.ca.us/cvpc

Safe Schools ... A Guide for Action

Chaos to Calm ... Creating Safe Schools

Shadows to Light ... A Guide to Child Abuse Reporting

COPPS ... Community Oriented Policing and Problem Solving

COPPS ... Building Safer Communities

Gangs ... Turning the Corner

Drug Free Zones ... Taking Action

Drugs and Youth ... The Challenge

Meth ... The Great Deceiver

Where Meth goes ... Violence and Destruction Follow!

Acknowledgments

The Attorney General's Crime and Violence Prevention Center gratefully acknowledges the many individuals who have contributed to *Law in the School* in the past and those who assisted in completing this edition, including:

Dave DeAlba	Special Assistant Attorney General, California Department of Justice
Lisa H. Ashley	Deputy Attorney General, California Department of Justice
John Burton	Executive Director, Student Support Services Fontana Unified School District
Jonathan R. Davis	Deputy Attorney General California Department of Justice
Beth Trinchero	Executive Fellow, California California Department of Justice
Mary Tobias Weaver	Assistant Superintendent/Division Director, Education Support Systems Division California Department of Education

Crime and Violence Prevention Center Staff

Kathryn P. Jett	Director
Tom Powers	Deputy Director
Patty O'Ran	Assistant Director
Steve Jefferies	Program Manager/Writer
Peggy Bengs	Editor
Jan Mistchenko	Graphic Designer
Oscar Estrella	Graphic Designer

In addition, the Crime and Violence Prevention Center gratefully acknowledges the assistance of the following individuals for their support and review of this publication: Shinita Bryson, Executive Secretary; Arlene Shea, Program Manager; and Linda Shimada, Administrative Assistant.

The center also wishes to acknowledge Wendy Alexander for her editorial and writing contributions.